SOUTHERN ESCAPADES
ON THE ROADS LESS TRAVELLED

Road Dog Publications was formed in 2010 as an imprint of Lost Classics Book Company and is dedicated to publishing the best in books on motorcycling and adventure travel.

ISBN 978-1-890623-49-4
Library of Congress Control Number: 2015955786

Worldwide distribution including
USA and Canada—www.nbnbooks.com;
UK, Australia, and New Zealand—www.nbninternational.com

An Imprint of Lost Classics Book Company

This book also available in e-book format at online booksellers. ISBN 978-1-890623-50-0

SOUTHERN ESCAPADES
ON THE ROADS LESS TRAVELLED

BY ZOË CANO

Publisher
Lake Wales, Florida

DEDICATION

To Lisa, Lulu, and Julia
and all those who believe dreams can come true

About the Author

Zoë Cano, whose name means "Life," is an adventurous traveller, writer, and photographer.

Born in Hereford, England, she moved to live and work in Paris for ten years before working in New York and, finally, Boston, with extended periods in Brazil and Asia for the international events and exhibition business.

She still travels extensively, often taking her beloved Triumph Bonneville motorbike.

Zoë now lives in London and is also the author of the highly successful *Bonneville Go or Bust—On the Roads Less Travelled.*

Prologue

Southern Escapades

Flying back from Los Angeles in 2012 from the crazy, summer road trip I'd just done, zig-zagging across America, and looking down at the massive continent below me, there was already a feeling deep inside me that it probably wasn't going to be the last trip of its kind!

Bizarrely, it was never intended, or even remotely envisaged, to write about the epic trip and produce the book, *Bonneville Go or Bust*. However, when I returned to London, with the Olympics just kicking off, there was a stream of messages from friends and people I didn't even know saying that, if the teasing blog snippets and tweets I'd done along the way were anything to go by, I really did have a story to tell!

I'd never written more than a school essay before and didn't have the slightest idea how to go about it, let alone get it published (not that that would ever happen!). Naively, but utterly determined, I sat down in my garden and tipped out from three very big Walmart bags all the dirty worn out coffee stained and marked up road maps, tatty torn leaflets on everything and nothing, postcards I'd promised to send and never did, and anything else interesting or strange I'd just kept as a souvenir to see if I could pull my stories from them. Just as importantly, I'd also taken more than a thousand photographs and, just looking at them, with their exact geographic locations, the vivid and unique memories thankfully weren't lost and came flooding back.

Under the warm shade of the old pear tree in my garden, I mulled over and questioned if I was even capable of telling a story. I was going to bare my soul and was already feeling sensitive on how people would react to it.

But as Mum so aptly put it at the time: "Darling, if nothing else, it'll be a nice little reminder for you to keep and look back on and for us to read when we've got nothing better to do!"

So bright eyed and bushy tailed, I got to it, and, for the next five months during every spare moment I had away from the nine-to-five job, I shut myself off from the world to slog away and write the story. Finally, as the spring daffodils showed their smiling faces, I was also smiling and ready to show it, or at least talk about it. But the rejections started coming back mercilessly from British publishers, and I was on the verge of maybe doing what my mum had said and using it as a door stop!

But the twist of fate comes when I'm contacted to give an interview with an American journalist following a motorbike chat forum we'd both been on. The trans-Atlantic interview took place and that's what opened the literary book doors! The very next day, I was contacted by a real book publisher on the East Coast in Florida who'd listened to the interview, liked what my story was about, and asked to see the manuscript! What?! Mine? Holy shit. This is crazy. I took a deep breath, pressed the send button on the laptop, and the manuscript disappeared into the ether.

Miraculously, and even more ironically, on the American holiday of the Fourth of July, I received a short, to the point, but very important message from Mike, of Road Dog Publications. "Hi, I've read your manuscript over the past forty-eight hours. I want to take it on. It totally fits with what we do and is ideally suited for the American market! Let's do a deal and get going with it!"

So, there you go. And seven months later a box arrived from the US, and I was holding one of the shiny, glossy books in my hands. Now that felt good.

And then it all started going kind of crazy and into what I can only describe as a quickly twisted throttle or accelerated overdrive. My good friends at Triumph's Jack Lilley invited me to be with them on their stand at the Triumph Live Show in the UK, where I did my very first book signings. That was all new to me. I'd never done anything like that before, and the simple fact that people actually wanted to buy and then have me sign them made me want to pinch myself that this was for real.

The momentum in 2014 didn't subside. Towards the end of it, I made the big decision to fly back over to America to attend a number of key shows for book signings and, yes, all on a motorbike! Triumph kindly provided a T100 Bonneville to help me get around and invited me to join them at the Barber Vintage Festival in Birmingham, Alabama.

I also finally met Mike, my publisher, and we joyfully concocted a plan to get back on the road, which would cover a totally new part of the United States to which I'd never been.

It was then, following this much shorter, but no less adventurous, trip that Southern Escapades came to life on the "roads less travelled."

It's funny, but this most recent trip down in the Deep South of the United States and covering more than 2,000 miles was very much like my initial trip across America. I didn't travel with the intention to write, but so much unexpected, funny and not so funny stuff happened along the way that it was all too good not to try to put pen to paper again!

So, here are some stories covering the lesser known parts of the beautiful Southeastern states of Florida, Alabama, and Georgia. Travelling the majority of it with me was my intrepid Road Dog companion and fellow traveller, Mike, who helped me discover these beautiful roads and hidden treasures.

TABLE OF CONTENTS

1

CREATING ANOTHER ROAD TRIP

Summer 2014

"Are you for real, Mike? It feels like only yesterday that I was coming back from the US!"

"Sure! Timing couldn't be better. We've done the hard slog this past year, got your crazy story out over on your side of the pond, and now in an ideal world all you need do is the same over here in the States. Seriously, I know money's tight but you'll never have another opportunity like this. So get your ass over and experience a bit of authentic Southern Hospitality on the roads less travelled down here!"

Strong and direct words, indeed, from my publisher, who I'd never met but had been communicating with on a regular basis for almost a year.

"God, it's tempting. When are you thinking?"

"Ideally? Let's think." I hear him laugh on the other end of the phone and in a split second replies, "Not a lot, to think about! I know this sounds crazy, but how about us doing a road trip and bike up from here in Florida to Birmingham, Alabama, for the big Barber Vintage Festival bike show in October at the famous racetrack? I've done that trip a number of times, and we'd take the smaller, more indirect roads, completely avoiding the major highways, which aren't that pretty anyway and are a hell of a bore!"

I hear the speed of his voice accelerate with animated excitement: "The roads from here up westward along the Florida coast on the Gulf side and up into Alabama are amazing. It's not your normal route to get up there. And, well, Alabama is definitely way different to anything you've seen elsewhere here across the country."

The enthusiasm continues, "And I know what! We could do a loop and travel back through Georgia to give you a real feel of the South. It would only be a couple of thousand miles there and back! So, just a night's stop over each way! What do you think?"

"Mmm, Umm, Mmm, well," is all I seem to reciprocate with on the other end of the phone line.

He continues, without mincing his words: "I'm sure there's a way we could get you to be there in some capacity, with maybe even Triumph for some more book signings. Your story would go over great there. That would be amazing. If we can't find a bike for you, I'd be happy to lend you my Bonneville, and I'd take my old 1968 Honda 350, although I'd need to do some serious tuning and maintenance work to it to get it roadworthy for that kind of distance."

I remember Mike previously saying he was a dab hand at mechanics, so that alone would definitely alleviate worries about any problems that may occur out on the road—something less for me to worry about.

Again, all he hears on the line from me is "Mmm, Umm, well, yes but..."

He persuadingly continues: "Come on. It would be fun. We can keep costs real low and take a tent and camp out on the trip there and back. I have friends throughout the Southern states, and there are guys from the Vintage Japanese Motorcycle Club, that I edit the club magazine for, who I'm sure would welcome and put us up in their backyards and..."

The idea of that accommodation option doesn't exactly appeal to me, and I quickly interject, "Mike, surely we couldn't camp out on this road trip." Half jokingly I add, "Where would I dry my hair to look presentable to your compatriots. Surely there must be another option?"

"Sure I have friends who also have floor space and spare rooms. Well, just an idea. Think about it. But you better do it quick."

Oh boy. Sorely tempting and exciting. Biking out with someone who knows the interesting lesser known routes and would take the lead, which would give me the time and luxury to appreciate and absorb the countryside and all the new places, without floundering with the maps for once. It would be a real holiday not being responsible for navigating and finding places to stay. I can handle that. Sounds great!

And, just like me, Mike is someone who doesn't use sat-nav but just good old fashioned road maps, so there may be lots of adventure in getting lost or finding new unexpected things along the way. Bring it on!

Mike hasn't had to do much to sell me the idea! But I'll need to find a solution for getting a bike, and this time there's only three months left to sort it all. My brain starts racing with ideas, and with two weeks still left from my annual vacation entitlement, I feel this crazy idea could somehow work. I need to, once again, escape and experience something new.

October 2014

"Flight BA 2039 from London is on time and has just landed," announces Orlando's echoey tannoy system.

Having never met Mike or his family, we've agreed to look out for each other at the arrival gates. He's already joked he'll be wearing one of his padded bike jackets. I tell him I'm the one with the biggest suitcase and a helmet bag swung over my shoulder.

I walk through Customs and immediately see a young, smiling boy, almost like a good looking younger brother of Harry Potter, come running up to me. Seeing my bike helmet, he enthusiastically grins like he's got it right and says a little shyly, "Hi! Are you the English girl coming to stay with us?"

I play along and put on a strong regal accent. "I guess I am. And who are you, Sir?"

"I'm Jacob, and Dad's over there," pointing to a man with a long tied-back ponytail and a cell phone attached to his ear, pushing tirelessly through a crowd of people pulling suitcases. "His friend has driven us over and is waiting for us outside."

Mike casually walks over and, with a broad, friendly grin, gives me a strong slap on the back. "Welcome to the States! Hey guys, let's get out of here quick and head back to Lake Wales. Shouldn't take us much more than an hour."

I immediately feel we're all going to get on like a house on fire, with Jacob now insisting he pulls my case for me. I'd asked what the kids liked and had made sure to bring a few surprises for them packed away in the case.

Speeding southwards down the night time highway to "I don't know really where," I feel we're already embarking on a major field trip with military precision, where my concentration cannot afford to lapse.

Shouting from his back seat to me in the front, Mike animatedly explains, "OK, Zoë, I've chatted with the guys at Fun Bike Center over in Lakeland, and they've said we can go pick up your T100 from them at 10 AM tomorrow morning. Triumph communicated and sorted it with them and requested a black one. Let's see what's been done. I'll bike, and you can pillion with me. Then we'll both bike back—a sixty mile round trip—prep them, pack, and be ready to leave at dawn the following day! How does that sound?"

"Phew! I'll let you know once I've had a good night's rest, but I'm glad someone knows what we're doing!"

2

A Land of Surprises

The sun shines through the window early the next morning and, without any blinds at the window, naturally wakes me up. Having somehow lost my watch briefly while unpacking in the dark last night, I have no idea what time it is. The house still seems asleep. I pull on my jeans and walk quietly barefooted along the creaky old dark wooden floorboards of this historical Southern house and out onto the long veranda that overlooks the school baseball fields.

The small road in front of the house is empty of any traffic, and there are just a few seagulls flying high up over the playing fields. I breathe in the warm air, listening to the quiet silence of this small community. But not for long. I hear distant hammering or the kicking of something in a garage next door. Someone must be up. I wander over.

I pop my head curiously into the garage, or what looks more like a workshop with all sorts of biking paraphernalia stacked on tables, piled on the floor, and hanging from every space on the walls, and see Mike diligently taking off the side bags from his Bonneville.

He's startled and turns round. "Hey, good morning! How did you sleep? Not too jet lagged or tired I hope, particularly after those beers we all also had last night. Andrea's already left for work, and the kids, Jacob and Tess, should be up soon and catching the bus to school. You know what? I'm sure Tess is going to take that book you gave her of Dr. Who, to school with her to make her buddies jealous. Talk about a fan of "The Doctor"! Did you see her eyes filled with delight when she opened it?" He chuckles and gets back to lifting the bike off the stand and wheeling it out.

I follow him out.

"And after we've had coffee, we can head out to Lakeland to pick up your bike. It's exciting! I went over there last week just to make sure all was in order when I was collecting some parts from them, and they seemed like everything was ready and they were looking forward to meeting you."

So, slightly caffeined out and with Mike getting on the bike, I carefully swing my leg over the seat of this coffee and cream lacquered (or that's how I'd describe the colour) beauty and hold my hands firmly on the back of the seat frame, trying to look like I do this all the time. Which I don't! Mike turns the key and starts the engine, and we're off.

At this stage, I have to say that, besides a one and only horrendous trip as a pillion many years ago along hundreds of miles of a rainy British motorway from London to the Lake District, I have to admit I'm not an expert in moving with a bike and rider. But Mike is already leaning nicely round the bends, past the baseball grounds, and a big lake, and I'm trying hard to keep in smooth motion with him and, above all, avoid bumping into him and crashing our helmets when he brakes! If he doesn't think I'm a good pillion, then he's surely going to start worrying about how competent I am in riding a bike!

We ride through the little town of Lake Wales, which I'd only caught glimpses of in the dark last night, but which I'm sure I'll get to see more of later on in the trip, over some bumpy railroad tracks, and almost immediately take a corner and sweep into a large car park.

"Gotta get some money from the bank before we leave tomorrow," and, with that, he gets off the bike and I follow him into a massive, high ceilinged, almost church-like, building of a bank. The place seems totally out of place in such a small town, and it's totally empty besides about twenty jacketed bank clerks quietly seated behind desks, looking curious, seeing a new face from out of town. Mike soon stuffs some cash into his inside jacket pocket, and we're off again.

It certainly wasn't the first time I'd been to Florida. In fact, it was probably the fourth or fifth time. Each trip before had just been to an anonymous hotel or exhibition centre in Orlando or Fort Lauderdale for business trips and, oh yes, when I was a kid on a Greyhound bus trip with my Dad. It had taken us all the way along the East Coast from New York to Miami. But the entire trip was in a cramped, window-locked bus, seated in the back with no real view, and only going on pre-organized trips with everyone else on the bus to massive tourist attractions like Disney and Cape Canaveral. And we always seemed to be on the main highway arteries—never away from those busy, congested main routes. Speed in getting to the many destinations on the itinerary, I understand now, was the priority.

So, I guess you could say, now was the first time I was really going to get a chance to get under the skin of Florida.

This trip, I know, was going to be totally different. I'd always imagined Florida to be very flat and everywhere inland monotonously boring, with very little eclectic scenery to speak of. But in almost a wink of an eye, we'd already climbed up a couple of hillsides covered with citrus groves, gone past half a dozen wild lakes of some substantial size, and along these back roads through beautiful, quaint little villages and farmsteads with cattle and horses contentedly grazing in lush green meadows.

With the warm air, that I've missed so much, now brushing past my bare arms, and the blue, blue skies, I really feel like I'm somewhere in the deepest South, as I start seeing what I only imagined were in Louisiana and Mississippi. Along the small, empty country roads on each side are old oak and cypress trees with masses of beautiful Spanish moss hanging from their branches—long beards swaying in the breeze. Truly Southern. I was starting to realize that we were in the South!

Mike prods me in the side with his elbow, and then I see him pointing to the moss laden trees and turning his index finger around and around, which I imagine means he wants to tell me something about them when we get a chance to talk. I make a mental note to remind him.

But we're soon at a busy city junction and hit Lakeland and East Memorial Drive, where the Fun Bike Center Motorsports outfit is located. I'm in for a surprise!

A shiny, black Bonneville T100 motorbike is already parked up outside the main entrance, and I have to do a double take! Next to it, on either side, are large waving flags with Triumph embossed on them, and next to the bike are three guys standing in a line, smiling and waiting to greet us—Elliott, Samer, and Nicholas are the head honchos here. We walk towards them, and I'm immediately taken by the arm and asked to stand between them while one of their colleagues films us as they hand the keys over to me. Wow! I didn't see that coming! We're then shown through their massive shop, which also sells Honda, Kawasaki, MotoFino, and Yamaha motorbikes and ATVs and a massive array of biking equipment for all tastes. I feel like I've been asked to do a royal tour!

Then walking around, Samer chirps up, "Hey, could we maybe ask you both for another photo opportunity?" An aquamarine and white Triumph Bonneville, with a beautiful retro rocket-shaped chrome side car, is in the middle of the showroom. I'm asked to sit on the bike, while Mike is relegated to squeezing into the sidecar. I can't help but giggle how surreal it all feels while just hoping Mike won't get stuck and us needing to pull him out!

We finally bid our farewells with promises that along the way we'll be sending them photos of the trip and we will have stories to tell them when we drop the bike off in two weeks.

I pull my helmet back on and, for the first time, start my bike up, which will be with me now to travel all the way up through the Southern states. I just can't wait. But not before I insist on riding it round the forecourt a few times just, as you could say, "to get used to it."

I smile, remembering a similar occasion sometime ago back in Boston, when I started the first trip. But Mike is already off, signalling to get out at the junction, and I'm quickly on his tail, following him back through the verdant little back roads. This is already great. It's wonderful not having to worry today about finding my way with new road maps and just simply having a good local person confidently leading the way.

I'm already sighing with a little relief. He doesn't seem to be riding like a macho maniac, and I'm starting to feel confident that I'll be able to keep up with him. To be honest, that's what I was worried about; that I wouldn't be able to ride fast enough and I'd get left behind and lost, or maybe he'd purposely be going more slowly than usual (and maybe getting a bit frustrated). What I do know is that I'm going to be totally at his mercy on this big ride up to Alabama. I haven't prepped the route because it's all been done at the last minute, due to Mike planning with his friends where we'll be stopping off and staying along the way. I do hope it works out OK.

It also feels like my stomach is calling for lunch. Mike must also be thinking along the same lines. Along more country roads, we head south to Frostproof. (Don't you just love the name?) At what feels like the middle of nowhere, we pull in and park the bikes up, right outside the epitome of an American family diner. The Christmas decorations and tinsel are still up around the windows, and, as we walk in, I notice film poster paraphernalia are all over the walls and people are in the booths contentedly eating massive homemade burgers and drinking from their equally massive Coca-Cola branded glasses.

We can do no better but order the same. I have to say that places like this, with such a relaxed feel, create natural curiosity. A couple at the next table have overheard us talking and can't help but ask where "Missy" is from!

"Well, Ma'am, I'm from London, that's London on the other side of the pond, not London, Texas!" They giggle like kids and continue biting into their burgers.

Our food arrives, and we're soon tucking in. All of a sudden, I have a shock in what I see walking in and take a second look. I discreetly nudge Mike over the table and look at him with incredulous open eyes. A couple of cowboys with Stetsons, well-worn cowboy boots, and dusty leather chaps take two bar stools. These have got to be the real thing, and they look like they've just jumped off their horses! They shout over to the guy behind the bar for two cold drinks.

"Mike! Have you seen those guys? I think they're real cowboys!"

"Hey, Zoë, come on! We're in the middle of cowboy country here. It's totally normal. Just east of us from our place in Lake Wales is the largest cattle ranch in the US!"

I blink in astonishment. "No! You've gotta be kidding! I rode through Texas and Oklahoma, and that's all you saw!"

Mike looks serious for once. "Why should I be joking? I promise you, the place is massive and is a well-kept secret. It's owned, I think, by the Church of Jesus Christ of Latter Day Saints!"

That rings a bell, reminding me of when I was in Salt Lake City. Are we talking about the Mormons?

Mike continues, "It's called Deseret," and with that he takes his phone and types in a few words. "Here you go. Listen to this. It's fifty by thirty miles wide and is definitely the largest in the world, not just here! Because of its size, with more than 42,000 mother cows, 44,000 calves, and 1,300 bulls the ranch has to be split into twelve operating units. Can you believe that? At Deseret, a typical cowboy usually manages more than a thousand cows, and they all work on horseback. There you go! The grasslands here are so abundant and fertile that that's pretty much all they eat, besides just a bit of stuff in the winter." He smiles and looks up from the phone. "That's also why you'll see so many steak houses here in the center of Florida. We'll have to take you to one of them before you leave."

"Great, give me good red meat anytime!"

"I was also thinking, to make the most of your time, that we could do another little interesting detour this afternoon to quickly show you more of the place before packing up to leave tomorrow."

"Sure. I'm all ears. What have you got in mind?"

"Well, I've gotta drop some tools off at Andrea's father's place. He lives on one of the canals into Crooked Lake, up the road from us. He just got a new pontoon boat that we can take out, and I'll show you some of the wildlife and things around there. Like the idea?"

Now that sounds good and very different. "Well, if you're sure, yes, of course. But have we enough time?"

"Yea, why not! Shouldn't take more than a few hours, and we'll be home before the kids get back from school. Then you can say you really have seen something out of the ordinary.

I'm keeping my mouth shut but there's at least one or two things out there that really will surprise you, if we see them!"

So, gulping down the rest of the meal and saying goodbye to the cowboys, we head back to the house, grab the tools, and bike on over to Crooked Lake. We park in the driveway of a lovely house, but out at the back is something spectacular. A beautiful canal waterway is lapping up at the bottom of the sloping green garden, and at the top of the slope as we walk out is an enormous covered swimming pool, covered with screened walls and ceiling. No one seems to be around, so we walk down to the deck on the waterfront that is shaded by a lovely wooden roof. A beautiful motor boat is moored alongside it and it's a type I've never seen before. It must be at least thirty feet long and is actually a specially designed boat for these lakes and can cope with the shallow canals.

"Believe me. You've got nothing to worry about. I can handle the boat. I'm a qualified skipper." Mike says reassuringly.

The afternoon is warm and hazy with, OK, maybe just a few heavy clouds out in the distance, but nothing major. Mike jumps into the skipper's seat, and I take a rotating cream leather seat. This feels like pure decadence, but probably something quite normal here. The mooring ropes are pulled in and the fenders pulled up and over into the boat. The engine comes to life, and we're soon motoring down the canal, through stretches of water covered totally in coloured water lilies. Large residential homes are dotted intermittently on each side of the grassy tree-lined banks. We come to the entrance of the lake—how beautiful. Not a single other boat is in sight. We and the wildlife have the lake all to ourselves.

Along the shoreline, before venturing too far out, are what look like marshlands, and there we already get a sighting of a family of great blue herons walking elegantly on their stilt like legs through these long water grasses. We quickly pick up some extra speed and bump out over the small waves. The lake is enormous, meandering ever further out into the distance.

After a while, Mike shouts over the sound of the engine, with me holding onto my seat trying not to slip off and trying to catch his words. "See how big this lake is and how it zigzags out and around? The Indian name of the lake is 'Caloosa,' meaning 'crooked.' Makes sense."

This is fun, and it's wonderful to see so much vast open water. All of a sudden the boat decelerates, and Mike points up to the sky. There, directly above, is an American Bald Eagle flying over. I estimate the wing span must be over two metres, and it looks enormous. Bald eagles are not actually bald; the name derives from an older meaning of "white headed" with the body being mainly brown and with a white head and tail.

Still trying to hear what Mike says, he continues. "Those guys are so opportunistic—they'll swoop down and snatch the fish from the water with their talons. This is a perfect place for them—large open waters, lots of food, and old trees for nesting."

After about forty minutes exploring the lake, we head back and enter one of the small canals. Perched on a piece of wood, peeping out of the water, is an Anhinga, also known here, but don't tell me why, as a "Water Turkey." Apparently, the wings are not waterproof like those of a duck, so, after diving for fish—and they can actually swim underwater—they must perch somewhere in the sun, extend their wings open, and dry them before going back into the water again, or they'll sink! With this one flapping his wings, it looks like he's doing just that.

We continue slowly motoring down the canal, when Mike suddenly stops the boat. "I don't believe it! This really is your day. Look just in front of the boat. Quick, before it disappears. Can you see a head? Now, can you see the back and tail? It must be about four feet long! It's just floating there!"

I wince my eyes looking carefully over the boat. "Oh. my god. It's a crocodile!"

Mike smiles patiently. "Well, actually it's an American alligator, or as they're usually called around here, "gators." They grow about a foot a year, so this one must be about four years old. Not bad. Florida does have saltwater crocodiles, but I've never seen one. They're pretty rare and only live in the very southern, isolated parts of the Everglades, near the salty edges of Florida Bay, which extends from the tip of Florida to the Florida Keys. So are you wildlifed out? Wanna head back for a beer at the house and get ourselves ready for the big day tomorrow?"

"Sure. So I guess we'll also be getting the bikes ready for that early start you mentioned tomorrow." Expecting a crazy hour, I pluck up the courage anyway and ask, sounding relaxed for any outcome, "So, what time do you reckon we'll be leaving?"

"Well, nothing bad. I'd say, if we can hit the road by seven, we'll avoid the morning rush commuter traffic heading to Orlando."

I reply, relieved, "That's good with me. I'll pack everything up on the bike tonight so we're ready to go. Sound like a plan?"

"Couldn't do better myself," smiles Mike. "It's gonna be a great first day, heading up along the coast to Panama City. My friends there are out of town, but their son is at the house, so we have the luxury of a room each, instead of a floor each! Everything is now planned to stay at friends' places, so I'm not even taking the tent, which is a first for me!"

I smile, realizing he may have taken seriously what I had said about the camping!

3

BACK ON THE ROAD

Lake Wales, Florida, to Panama City, Florida

392 miles

The sun starts to appear over the trees in the backyard. It must be about six'ish. Busy noises are already coming from the kitchen, and the glorious smell of coffee literally filters through to me. But I've been awake for a while now contemplating the day ahead and maybe palpitating just a small bit on not really knowing what to expect. But the adrenalin rush overtakes that. I'm excited about taking this intrepid trip up to Alabama with my Road Dog! And fab stuff—Mike's insisted that he's going to be managing the route, so no massive planning needed from me. I can literally just sit back and enjoy the ride.

Although maybe not totally! I was diligently given a road map of Florida just last night and told to take a good look at it and put it in my tank bag, which Mike jokingly said I could use to simply track where we're headed or use if I loose him! Fun. No responsibilities besides not getting left behind! What would I do then? We have decided, just to be safe, that I'll take the addresses of where we're staying each day so if, God forbid, I did get lost, I could at least find my way there. But hell, hang on, it is the twenty-first century! We've got cellphones! I'm just worrying unnecessarily. But I guess that's me all over, worrying for the smallest of things.

I put on my biking gear, the usual, jeans, T-shirt and boots and walk into the kitchen, which is now empty except for the coffee. I pour some into a mug and thirstily drink it up. Then I carry my tank bag and helmet out to the garage.

Mike has already wheeled both bikes out onto the grass at the front of the house. His is fully packed. I can somehow feel his impatience in wanting to get started.

"Morning Zoë. How are you feeling? Are we ready to go? The weather's looking pretty good today, with no expected rain. We should make Panama City, without any delays, by early evening. I've checked the bikes. Yours looks OK, and it's good that you have that windscreen they gave you. Although I think when we get up to Barber we'll take it off to create more refinement for you," he says, smiling.

He continues smiling mischievously, "I suggest that you place this massive pop-up panel you brought over from London to use at the show on the top of your bag on the seat. We can strap everything tightly down. I've got loads of extra bungee cords. It should all be alright, but you'll need to keep an eye on it that it keeps centered and doesn't slide off. It must be at least three feet long! People are gonna wonder what it is—maybe a gun!"

With everything tied down, helmets fastened, and triple checking my phone is with me in my tank bag, and with keys in hand, I insert them, and the engine comes to life. Both Bonnevilles start up immediately. That's one thing I've noticed riding in the US. When the weather's good it's never a problem to start up the bikes. Never having to deal with a freezing cold engine.

So this is it. Another new road trip and adventure beginning today and with Mike my travelling buddie, who jokingly refers to himself now as my Road Dog. A term I'd never heard of before. But trawling through the urban dictionary, it just means a good travelling companion. I'm cool with that. It's been rare for me to do long trips with others, but for this ride through the Deep South, with not a lot of time to get up to Birmingham and not one of the safest areas, I feel doing it with someone I trust and who knows these unknown back roads through Alabama is going to help make it a hell of a lot easier and a load more fun.

Mike looks over his shoulder to me and nods his head, as if to say, "OK, we're off," but not before pointing to the sky. A large bird, almost the size of an eagle but with a whitish chest and light speckles on its huge wings, hovers over us for a split second then flies and lands on the top of one of the ball field light poles, where a large nest seems to be precariously balanced.

"One of our neighbours. There's two ospreys here at the moment, and they're becoming fairly common to see around here. These are birds of prey, too, but it's funny they don't mind nesting in man-made structures, like our baseball poles and towers. That bald eagle we saw yesterday is more particular. He'll only nest in natural locations, like the tops of pine trees. Go figure! OK. Let's get going. We'll grab some breakfast or something to eat when we're out of the city congestion around Lakeland and are on Route 98."

I then see Mike diligently kick into first gear and slowly ride down the grassy slope out onto the road, but not before the kids, still in their PJs, who've no doubt heard the bikes being started up, come running out of the house to wave us goodbye.

I also smile and wave goodbye, then pull my tinted visor down and duplicate what Mike has just done and bike out onto the quiet road.

Here we go! My bike is purring, and I stroke its gleaming brand new black tank. We head out of sleepy little Lake Wales, with a population of just around 12,000, and past its beautiful houses overlooking the town's almost namesake, Lake Wailes. Yes, that's right, another spelling! Apparently the original surveyor of the land here at the end of the nineteenth century was Sidney Irving Wailes, who changed the name of the lake then known as Watts Lake to Lake Wailes. But the city of Lake Wales established near the lake only in 1911-1912 was planned by the Lake Wales Land Company, so both spellings stuck.

We ride over the same bumpy railway tracks that we'd gone over yesterday to pick up the bike, and I see Mike totally standing up from his seat on his foot rests and looking at me in his mirror, probably thinking I should have done the same. Next time!

With a large part of the Florida road map spread out in front of me in the tank bag, I'm seeing that Lake Wales is pretty much in the centre of this subtropical peninsula, between the Atlantic and the Gulf of Mexico. Our main road today will be US Route 98, hanging a left up along the Gulf of Mexico coast and then hugging that coastline for a couple of hundred miles, all the way up to Panama City. Bring it on!

Without exaggerating, I'm in my element. A warm breeze, no heavy waterproof gear, the sun shining brightly, and easily keeping up with my Road Dog, who is by now keeping up a steady speed of 55-60 miles per hour. Again re-tracing the by-roads up to Lakeland that we took yesterday, the breeze in the air is gently blowing through the Spanish Moss-laden trees. I remember being told only last night that this wispy natural material has been incredibly useful. In the 1900s, it was unbelievably used for padding the very first car seats and up until more recently for stuffing traditional voodoo dolls!

We're quickly out and through Lakeland, which resembles one massive chain of outlets along a busy major highway, and heading northwestwards to the tropical coastline.

In just over an hour, or fifty-seven miles to be exact, on what seems still like a main artery of a highway, Mike signals right and turns into a massive McDonalds. I'm glad he's getting priorities right.

Taking his helmet off, Mike utters, "Man, I can't wait to get a coffee and something to eat. They also do pretty good pancakes here if you're interested! Your first meal out on the road has to be a Mickey D's!"

We walk into a huge place, where the counters are heaving with food and the capped and white-aproned people behind them are busily flipping food and pouring drinks big enough to sink a ship! Mike orders what he calls a "breakfast sandwich" but in reality is their Egg McMuffin. I opt for bagels and pull some fruit out from my bag. The day before, having previously experienced the lack of fresh food when out on the road, I'd grabbed the opportunity to go to the local supermarket and stock up on some healthy bananas and apples, which I'd then stuffed into my side bags for easy access. I knew, as is current proof, that I might just be eating quite a bit of fast food due this time to our restricted budgets!

We sit down, with both helmets on the table next to us, and I can see Mike hungrily scoffing the food down in a matter of minutes. While he's also downing his coffee just as quickly, I smile and can't help but say, "Hey, Mike. Don't get me wrong, this place is great, but looking at the maps always makes you think places so are much closer. Looking at it last night, I was thinking we might have had breakfast on a beach overlooking the sea somewhere. But it still looks like we're some way off from seeing any coastline."

With his mouth still full, unable to talk, but his eyes wide open, he simply nods in agreement.

And then we're off again, through more fairly congested roads. All of a sudden, we rapidly, and perhaps too quickly, come to some traffic lights, which immediately turn green. Mike puts his indicator on at the last minute to make a sharp left turn. I start to panic, not quite knowing how to handle the bike with this manoeuvre, and, instead of going down a gear to better take the bend, I get confused and accelerate! Shit. Shit, Shit. I can feel the bike's wheels slipping, and I feel I'm going to be a gonna, falling off and potentially injuring myself already on the first day!

Miraculously, and don't tell me how, but me or the bike or both somehow re-balance, and besides a bit of wobbling, I keep on and the bike keeps a hold of the road. God, that was close, not good, and I can feel my hands shaking a bit. Once again, I'm not selling myself that I'm a perfect biker—far from it—and probably, well actually, definitely, a little nervous in quick, difficult manoeuvres, but that was close. It happened so damn quick that I don't think Mike even noticed anything, unless he's being incredibly discreet, polite, or simply embarrassed by my ineptitude. He's probably thinking who the hell he's accepted to go out on this trip with! Moments like that make me respect what I'm doing even more. I pat the bike and almost thank it that it had been a good boy.

We steadily continue navigating towards Brooksville. It's there, this time waiting at some red lights to cross a busy junction, that I look into my mirror. They're coming up fast behind us! There's got to be at least five or six guys on beautiful cafe racer bikes, with pure retro coolness oozing from them. They've also got bags and tents packed on the bikes, so they must be heading out somewhere. Maybe they're also heading up to The Barber Vintage Festival, where these kinds of guys will be hanging out at the Ace Corner, overlooking the racetrack.

But we've got another six hundred miles until we get there, and we're not exactly taking the most direct route—surely not! Maybe they're just taking a few days off and going to the beach or some music festival closer to home here in Florida. They all come to a sudden halt, surrounding us both with courteous nods and smiles. The light turns green, and they're immediately off! "Come on Mike," I'm thinking, "let's race on with them!" But they're soon out of sight and sound, except for the rubber marks left on the road.

So come on! When are we going to see the sea? Tempting names like Crystal River, Otter Creek, and Cedar Key whizz past us, names that make me just want to yell out, "Hey let's just go and check them out!" Thankfully the road is definitely getting less congested, and may I say, a little narrower.

With a hundred and fifty miles already under our belts, we reach the little town of Chiefland and pull into an empty, and aptly named, gas station called Marathon to fill up for the first time. New places always bring new things to see, and this place is no exception. Keeping my eyes open, I'm already smiling when I walk up to the counter to pay. On the window is pasted a small notice simply saying: "Free ride in a Police Car if you shoplift from this store—compliments of your Police Department." How polite!

We continue through the heat of the morning, which must already be in the 80s F, northwards on Route 19/98 until we get to the intersection at Perry. Then it's finally due west, hugging the coast on Route 98, or as the locals know it as the Big Bend Scenic Byway Coastal Trail. This beautiful, quiet coastline is full of inlets, estuaries, national parks, and state forests.

We cross a few small river bridges through the green Apalachicola National Forest, but it's not until we get just past Panacea and cross over the massive estuary of Ochlockonee Bay that I start to catch glimpses of the beautiful Gulf of Mexico and its sandy beaches. Joy. The visual senses of looking out to sea seemed to have gone up a couple of notches of amazement!

This is just too good to keep going, and I wave my arm frantically up and down to let Mike see I want to slow down and stop. He finally notices what I'm trying to do and indicates stopping just opposite Alligator Point and Alligator Harbor Aquatic Preserve and shouts over saying, "Let's get the bikes down that slope and park up by the sea. The wheels and our tootsies can take a feel of the water. The water here on the Gulf side should be a lot warmer than over on the Atlantic."

We carefully and very slowly ride the bikes right down to the warm, sandy beach, just a few yards from the quiet rippling sea. The hazy, hot sunlight somehow makes the horizon look slightly misty. Large cypress trees stand by the waterside, and a couple of older guys are quietly seated in the trees' shade holding long fishing rods, whose lines have been thrown way out to sea. If you have to wait for a long time for a fish to pull the line, this definitely has to be one of the best places around. I'm sure they agree with that.

Believe it or not, this is the very first time I'm trying to stand a bike on sand. And a heavy bike—all 450lbs, or 200 kilos, of dry weight, and I've got lots of luggage on it! So, with the weight of the bike and the softness and instability of the ground beneath, I have a deep feeling and worry that the bike could possibly tip over. Not this time! Road Dog to the rescue! Mike efficiently and immediately sees my dilemma and kindly rummages through his tank bag. He hands me a plastic disc, the size of a round beer mat, to put under the foot side stand to keep it from further sinking into the soft sand.

"Hang on there. Just jam this onto the sand and rest the stand on it. It'll do the trick. I was given some free ones by the Vintage Japanese Motorcycle Club at a show I recently attended. You can keep it, if you like, for future beach combing expeditions."

And so, for the first time, I don't have to worry about something happening that shouldn't with the bike and its consequences, like it falling over now and me being totally useless in getting it back up! Because now I have someone who'll help me. That makes me feel good. Again, the big question is if I was travelling on my own, would I have gone down to the beach with the bike? Probably not!

It's a quiet place and it would have been quite easy to throw a blanket under one of those cypress trees and have a little siesta, but we still have more than a hundred miles to cover, and with, apparently, even prettier places along the way.

I walk over to the bike and try and pull it upright from the sand. It's a bit stuck with the added weight of the luggage, and, to tell the truth, I'm not that confident on riding it back up the sandy hill onto the main road.

"God, Mike, I'm sorry. You did insist we bring them down to the seashore. Could you maybe ride it up over the dune back onto the road?'

"Sure. I do that every day," he says laughing.

Rather him than me. I throw him the keys, and he slides from side to side across the sand but at least manages to stay on the bike and navigate the sandy slope, which I would have probably found extremely difficult and stressful.

We continue hugging the flat, pretty coastline along quiet, small country roads until very soon we reach the beautiful unspoilt places of Lanark Village and Carrabelle, where wooden, stilted homes stand on white sandy beaches between shaded pine trees, just a few yards from the road. I see a handful of pelicans flying over. Paradise!

Further along the Scenic Coastal Trail to Eastpoint, which, once again, takes us across a massive waterway, we reach lovely

Apalachicola, still the home port for oyster harvesters and shrimpers. In fact, the majority of Florida's oysters come from this bay and the start of the Emerald Coast that goes up past Panama City.

I'm still really trying to get used to biking with someone else. I hope I'm OK and not creating too many unforeseen problems for Mike. The places I'd have stopped at to maybe take a quick photo or breathe in the atmosphere we ride past, and, without intercom and the smallest underlying phobia of getting lost, I prefer to stick in close eyesight to him at all times.

I'm not complaining. Far from it! I'm over the moon with this wonderful route. This certainly wouldn't have been the normal, direct way to Birmingham, Alabama, and I'm so pleased about that!

A few miles farther, we arrive at Port Saint Joe, another little place off the beaten path in a sheltered bay of scenic beauty and well known for its annual Scallop Festival and plentiful supplies of fresh seafood from its offshore fishing expeditions.

Very soon leaving these quaint, unspoilt places and heading further north along the coast, I can feel the call of urban civilization coming to get us again. Well, maybe not that bad, but riding through Mexican Beach, seeing the white beaches within touching distance, the area starts to look slightly more built up and commercialized, with shops and bars. Along this seafront, I feel I'm just about to see fake pink flamingos standing on one leg in the gardens opposite with precisely coiffed blond older women jogging along the board walks with brightly coloured yellow or purple poodles in tow!

We're approaching the outskirts of Panama City. Now this does feel like a big place, and I'm glad we're getting here just before nightfall. This has been a massive, bigger than expected day and at some points quite scary! Yep, a sweet four hundred miles!

I'm pretty tired and dying for a good hot shower, a cold beer, and maybe some seafood in some kind of beach shack.

But initial impressions are a little disappointing. We pass by what looks like massive industrial factories with billowing steam coming out from big towers, an air force base, then over a large bridge. Mike finds a place to stop on the side of the road and folds over his map, looking intently at it. He'll definitely need to use his road map reading skills to find the place we'll be staying at tonight, which I've been told is somewhere in one of the quieter residential districts.

He nods, and we're off again, and now with no view of the sea anymore. Besides the little I've seen so far, and will hopefully see later in the evening and before we leave early in the morning, Panama City is centrally located along this beautiful one hundred mile Emerald Coast we've been travelling up today, which, I'm told later, is more colloquially known as the "Redneck Riviera!"

Redneck Riviera is also the title of a song by Tom T. Hall of this region. I love the lyrics:

> *"Gulf Shores up through Apalachi-cola*
> *They got beaches of the whitest sand*
> *Nobody cares if gramma's got a tattoo*
> *or Bubba's got a hot wing in his hand.*
> *On Highway 98 I got a ticket*
> *Something I ain't never understood*
> *If driving a convertible is topless*
> *Why can't I ride my Harley in the nude?"*

Then we're finally off Route 98, which I can't believe we've been on in one form or another all day long, we start seeing a labyrinth of small residential streets. Mike quickly signals left (I'm ready this time!), enters a tree lined empty street with small, some rundown, houses, and finally turns the ignition off. We've arrived. It's a one storey wood painted house with a covered terrace running around the front and a massive back yard we bike around and back out again with enormous workshops and garages.

The vegetation out front is only what I can describe as "tropical," of the big, shiny, leathery leaf variety. I park up beside him and look in the mirror and then at him. Besides being a bit dirty, my face has turned a nice sunny red brown and Mike's has just got even darker. Hopefully, I'll catch up soon. There's nobody running out to "meet and greet us with a cold beer," so we pull our bags off and heave them up the few steps onto the terrace. The front door is unlocked. There's total silence as we knock and walk in.

"Hi there. Is there anyone home?"calls out Mike.

Still nothing. We walk towards the kitchen, but I'm sure I can hear something like shooting coming out from the room next to it. I stare seriously over at Mike. He coughs slightly and bravely walks towards the door, pushing it delicately open. A young guy with earphones must be playing some kind of killer computer game, with the noise of guns and screams resonating from the speakers and at the highest volume. He wouldn't have known if we'd shouted or screamed for him from the kitchen next door.

He casually brushes the long hair from his eyes, looks up from popcorn and cigarette butts that are scattered everywhere, and smiles very calmly. "Hey Mike, wattya doin' dude? Wanna hang here or get some air?"while lighting a new cigarette.

This is Andrew, our host for the evening and the son of Mike's father-in-law's nephew and niece, who are currently out of town. To be fair to Andrew, he had been expecting us for a while, ever since leaving his shift earlier that afternoon at the local Walmart. Without further to do, I can see this is going to be a pretty casual "stay over," so I politely ask the most important thing. "Hey Andrew, any problem in me using the shower? Been a long, hot day!"

He smiles and casually replies, "Sure. Sure. Do what you need to do. The shower is through that door, and your room is on the other side of the hallway. Mike, you can use the floor here or Mom and Dad's room!" I wonder what he'll choose!

Coming out feeling refreshed, it looks like Mike has the evening sorted. "There's a great little place downtown that

you just have to know about called "Billy's Steamer & Oyster."
Andrew says it's the real thing here, and he's gonna drive us
all over. That way you and I can have a beer! Sound good?
Oh, by the way, I hope you don't mind, but we're also going
to drive past Walmart so I can pick up some socks that I can
get at a special discount with Andrew working there. So let's
get going."

We jump, or rather, climb up into a massive black truck,
and loud acid house music is immediately turned on to
maximum deafening volume. The truck careers out of the
pitch dark driveway, and I find it hard to believe how it can be
driven without hands at the wheel! One hand is using a cell
phone, and the other is eating more popcorn. I'm just glad I'm
belted in and Mike is within proximity at the front to quickly
grab the wheel if the need arises!

With Andrew banging his hand on the wheel to the beat of
the music, he shouts out, "OK, guys, I'm gonna whizz round
and show you a bit of the place. We'll head down to the beach
strip where the parties happen all the time. This is the biggest
resort here in the Panhandle, with hotels and stuff going on
for about twenty-five miles. You'll see why it's called Miracle
Strip. Crowds come in for the Spring Break. It gets crazy!"

He's about right. It seems a little bit like a brash postcard
sort of place, full of hotels and amusement parks but next to
what looks like a beautiful sandy beach.

Mike is quick to compensate for what I've just seen
and heard. "I have to add that being a boat skipper and
knowing a bit about the sea around here, Panama City is
also nicknamed the 'wreck capital of the south.' It's a really
famous diving destination in the Gulf. Besides the natural
reefs, it's got masses of artificial dive sites created from
wrecked boats, which make it one of the best places in the
Gulf for diving. And between here and going westwards to
Perdido Key, they've got to be some of the most beautiful
beaches in Florida. There may be masses of people here in
the summer, but the Gulf waters here can stay nice and warm

right up until November. So there you go boys and girls for your classroom lecture today!"

We jump off the brightly lit strip and head down a quieter street and into an almost deserted car park. I'd been told that late at night Walmart is like walking into another world. The people you don't normally see just seem to appear there. Andrew quickly takes us to the "extensive and cheap selection of socks" department where Mike grabs a set, I'm sure without even looking at the size, or maybe they're all the same! Andrew then guides us speedily back to the till, but not before I've seen a few people looking like they're wearing pyjamas pushing their trolleys and one guy reading magazines with red lipstick on!

Although it's late, we don't mind. Sitting at the bar at Billy's with its hard wooden floorboards and wood shavings, listening to soft rhythm and blues music, watching plates piled high with shrimp, lobsters, and every conceivable sort of seafood going past us and cold tap beer being poured like there's no tomorrow, you could say I'm feeling pretty good. No, let's re-word that! I'm already feeling like I'm in a little part of paradise down here in the Deep South.

4

COTTON PICKING GOOD!

Panama City, Florida, to Leeds, Alabama

346 miles

We quietly creep out of the sleeping house, well before
Andrew has even woken up, and carrying the bags to the bikes
are greeted by a cool, misty morning. The tropical plants out
at the front are all covered in dew, as well as the bikes.

There is total quietness in this little residential road
except for some hens picking up grains on the road side and
disappearing back into the mist.

I take out my cloth from my side bag and wipe the seat dry
and hand it to Mike. "So, did you have a good night's rest? I
just crashed out as soon as my head hit the pillow."

"Yea, pretty much me, too. I did speak to Andrea, though,
to tell her we'd arrived safely without any mishaps."

I think to myself, "Well, there could have been even more theatre, like me almost falling off a couple of times round that curve at the intersection and down that sand dune." But I keep that to myself!

"OK Zoë. this is gonna be an interesting day. We're soon going to be reaching the Alabama border in an hour or two and, don't worry, you won't need to show your passport. I figure it's about seventy or eighty miles as the crow flies, but we'll try and get off onto the smaller roads as soon as we get out of the city here. Then it'll be zig-zagging up to Birmingham. Is there anything you wanna try and see along the way besides the back of me and the bike?" He says, smiling.

A big question. Yes we could go to Selma, Montgomery, and maybe into Birmingham, but there's really not enough time and they're not directly where we're going. Probably best to just go with the flow with Mike's plans. So I politely reply, "All sounds good. I'm just absorbing it all and am open to seeing new things, which will probably be everything. I'm chilled and happy there's no strict agenda today."

I then blurt something out which really would be cool and potentially feasible: "If we could get to see some cotton fields here in the Deep South that would be good. But is it even the right time of the year or has it all been harvested?"

"I guess it still must be. They really are quite an interesting sight. I remember travelling through Alabama and Mississippi a few years back, and the fields were just covered in white all over, like snow had fallen. I'll keep an eye out as soon as we cross the border. I'll also look out for a half-decent place where we can stop for breakfast. Should be some OK places the further we get out of town. I'll make sure it's not another McDonalds!"

With both bikes loaded up again, and without forgetting to put a small note on the kitchen table to thank Andrew for our crazy drive with him last night, we both do Ueys back out onto the main road. With not much choice in how we leave Panama City, we take the large Florida State Route 77 all the way to Crystal Lake and then onto the smaller Florida 279 due north.

These small roads in North Florida are beautiful, green and hilly and nothing remotely like I would have associated with Florida. Thirty-six miles into the day, with the temperature slowly rising, allowing me to take my fleece off and just wear the T-shirt, we approach a little place called Vernon and spot cute Dee's Restaurant. It looks like the neighbourhood family-run diner. Lots of cars and trucks are parked up outside, so that must be a good sign that it's popular and well frequented by the locals. We like that. Even more interestingly are three Harleys parked near the main entrance. Walking past them, I notice they're also loaded with bags and camping stuff. I wonder where they're going?

We push the door open and walk up to the counter, to see the walls covered in animal trophies. This area is obviously a place for hunting. We follow a friendly girl in a white apron and smiling face to our booth. I grasp the menu to see what's on offer. Not bad. This will do. We both order full plates of fried eggs "sunny side up," bacon rashers, hash browns, and toast, and I add tomatoes to my order. The girl immediately comes back doing what I love so much in America—immediately filling our big mugs with lots of coffee and coming quickly back again to top it up. Heaven. The place is buzzing, with the girl and her white apron being literally run off her feet, with lots of people looking like they're just about to go off to work or back down to the farm and all catching up on the local gossip.

I discreetly look round the small room, which probably has no more than fifteen other tables, trying to identify who the other bikers parked up front could possibly be, as there doesn't really seem to be a group of guy bikers here. Ruminating this thought, I pop up with an idea while I'm finishing off my eggs and wiping the plate clean with some toast.

"Mike, while you're finishing off, I'm going to pop back outside and put some of my flyers on the seats of those three

Harleys to show where I'm going to be in these next few weeks. You never know. They may be headed up to Birmingham, too!'

Mike frowns and cautiously looks at me, hesitating before he speaks, putting his words together in the most diplomatic way. "Well, be careful, 'cause guys around here don't much like their bikes being touched."

"Hey Mike! What could I do wrong? It's just a friendly gesture. I'm sure it will be fine, and I'll be discreet. See you in a bit."

So I walk back out and look around. There's nobody outside. I walk towards the three enormous, expensive-looking, shiny Harley bikes and pull out three little pieces of paper from my jacket pocket which I'd made up back in London simply to tell people where I'd be in the US signing the book. I'm feeling a bit shy and awkward in doing this for the first time, but I guess there's always a first time in anything and sure as hell no one else is going to do it for me.

I walk to the first bike and put the card under the strap on the seat. With extra confidence, I walk over to the next and put another card, this time carefully balanced on the handlebars, and walking to the last and largest of the bikes, I suddenly hear a menacing scream and a large fist banging from the window inside. It looks like the window is going to get broken! It must be one of the biker guys.

Before there's anything more I can do, a big white bearded, leather-clad guy comes running out to confront me. Now I'm going to have to say something pretty damn quick. But I've got nothing to say. I just smile nervously up at him.

"Oh, geez!" he says in an almost deflated but deep and relieved tone, "I thought those guys had come back to tamper with the bikes. We'd already shouted them away once. They looked suspicious."

"I'm really, really sorry. I obviously don't know the biking etiquette here, although I was warned! Truly, all I really wanted to do was give you a bit of information on where I'll be, as we're going up to the Barber show."

His glaring eyes begin to soften, and his straight face breaks into a small smile. "Hey, you're a Brit. I went to London once a long time ago. We're going up to the Barber Festival, too! Are those your two Triumphs we saw come in earlier? Nice bikes."

"Yes. We've just come up from Panama City earlier this morning."

He nods and, with that, walks over, holds his hand out to shake mine, continuing. "Hey, we're from there, too. I'm Harry. I'm here with my son and his daughter. Mary-Lee has only just started biking, and we all thought it would be a great family trip to all head up through Alabama and camp up at the show."

"Again, I'm really sorry. I'm Zoë. Maybe we'll see you there. I'll be with Triumph on their main stand so come and check us out."

"Cool, we sure will! I can't believe we're all going up. There are some beautiful roads up there to explore that we wanna show Mary-Lee. Make sure your partner does the same."

With that, we both walk back in and everyone gets introduced. Mike and I are being treated like long lost family members. "Now. don't forget," Harry says handing over a business card. "If you have any problems you now have our phone numbers, and, if you're coming back through Panama City, you're more than welcome to stay."

Mike politely interjects. "That's great, but we'll be heading east through Georgia on the way back. But it's always useful to have contacts on the road. The same goes for us." He smiles, also handing over his business card, relieved, I'm sure, that the small misunderstanding got smoothed out.

With that potential little fiasco sorted and out of the way, we wish each other safe trips, and we and the two Bonnevilles are soon back out on the road. That was a frightening lesson I won't forget in a hurry.

Just another thirty miles along Florida Route 79 with the sun now fully up and not a hint of any more morning mist that

I was having to continually wipe off the visor this morning, we've crossed over the major eastbound Interstate Highway 10, which goes all the way from Jacksonville on the east coast of Florida to Los Angeles on the west coast of the US. Soon, I find ourselves making an obligatory stop in the middle of nowhere. The road is empty, and green trees and long grassy verges line the road. Mike enthusiastically points to a sign, indicating that I ride the bike over to it. I smile and comply with his request. A large green sign announces, "Welcome to Alabama the Beautiful. Governor Robert Bentley."

A souvenir picture is taken of me pointing up to the state border sign with the blue cloudless skies above it. With nicknames like the "Heart of Dixie" and "The Cotton State," what do I think of the little I know and perceive about Alabama without being too blinkered and prejudiced? Well, I've been told and read that it's probably one of the poorest states in the US, with a history and unimaginable stories of slavery and racism.

During the first half of the nineteenth century, cotton and slave labour were central to Alabama's economy. The state also played a key role in the American Civil War, with its state capital, Montgomery, the Confederacy's first capital. Following the war, segregation of blacks and whites prevailed throughout much of the South. So I'm also envisaging seeing along the way a lot of poor and impoverished places with very little money. To add further to these issues, in the mid twentieth century, Alabama was at the centre of the American Civil Rights Movement and home to such pivotal events as the Montgomery Bus Boycott and the peace protest walk with Doctor Martin Luther King from Selma to Montgomery. These sort of heart-wrenching images I'd previously seen when I visited the Civil Rights Museum in Memphis. Will I still see any form of open racism, as, surely, when places have no money, segregation in major ways takes hold.

I also imagine that not a lot happens, that it's unbearably hot in the summer and cold in the winter. I think they even get a bit of snow! I don't think the population is big, either, in fact, with just under five million it's less than half that of its neighbouring state of Georgia, which has over ten million people. Will I see a lot of Confederate flags? Are they even allowed? Does the Ku Klux Klan still exist? They must be religious, with more than half of the population going to church! What do you eat in Alabama?

But, with my love of music, this has got to be the place to hear it, which I'm adamant to do. The Deep South is where the majority of musical roots came from. From the field slaves' "undiluted soul" Gospel music to blues, soul, and rhythm and blues, I get the impression we'll be hearing a lot of it. I've also planned something pretty major on that front while we're in Birmingham, and I just hope that one works out!

We carry on the same road, but which has now been renamed Alabama Route 167, and shortly pull over at Hartford to fill up. These are real Southern country roads with harvested fields of crops on either side, but, apparently, nothing that remotely looks like cotton. I can see Mike continuing to diligently look on either side of the road into the fields, trying to look out for something white.

It's true to say that, since entering Alabama, things feel like they've dramatically changed. There's hardly any traffic on the roads, and the pace feels a lot slower riding through the small towns. It looks, without doubt, a lot poorer than its affluent neighbour we've just left. I remember feeling just the same when I left Colorado and entered New Mexico on the last trip.

Amazingly, just another few miles or so further up the road, a small T-junction appears, and Mike signals confidently left. I'm curious at what he could be doing, but not for long. He parks up on the side of a field and there, as far as the eye can see, are white fluffy bobbles making the whole landscape look almost white. These are the cotton fields of the Deep South.

We ride onto the grass in front of the fields, and, getting off the bike, I walk towards the cotton, which surely has got to be gathered very soon. The other fields we'd passed had already been harvested. I pluck a piece of cotton off the shrub's woody stem and roll it between my fingers and pull it to feel its texture—so soft. Inside the blossomed ball of cotton, I feel a small protective capsule, or boll, from where the cotton's just popped out. I put it into my pocket.

Pulling a bottle of water out of his bag and offering me a drink, too, Mike says, "By tomorrow this whole white area will probably have disappeared and been harvested. We're very lucky."

With the bikes on the grassy verge of the cotton fields and being engrossed in taking some pictures, I'm distracted by suddenly hearing heavy duty engines and horns being blown to attract our attention. It's the Harley family who've just noticed us in the middle of these fields, and they're also waving enthusiastically at us, but they're soon out of sight. Hopefully, we'll see them again in Birmingham.

Amazingly, along and up through Alabama, this will be the only place we see the cotton ready to be picked. The weather is perfect—not too hot. We turn up onto US Route 29 at Troy, seeing signs along the way for Montgomery. Passing the small place of Banks, along this isolated road we see Black farm hands walking along the roads, lined with wooden dwellings and homes that look impoverished. It's getting hotter, and my throat is dry. Just up the road, we stop at "The Store," a simple, corrugated-roofed, almost temporary looking, white shed structure to buy water. It doesn't seem like a hell of a lot goes on around here.

Out at the front, before walking in, under the shaded porch area, are what I can only describe as three massive, over-sized, wooden white rocking chairs. In fact, with closer inspection, one is a double rocker. Seriously, each one could fit at least two of me!

Walking back out with just our bottles of water, I notice a Black guy is now seated quietly on one of these rockers, eating a few crackers. I'm fascinated. What's his story? He doesn't look like he's got much else to do or has much besides his biscuits. His clothes are old and oversized, wearing a torn Los Angeles basketball T-shirt, with dirty jeans and trainers. He's been looking at the bikes from the shade and probably thinks, although it's far from the truth, that we're wealthy travellers. I have a strong urge to make just a small effort and so walk up to him and sit down next to him. Strangers can be friendly, too, and so I spontaneously put out my hand to shake his. There must still be so many racial barriers here. He simply leans over and smiles and warmly shakes mine. He offers me one of his last remaining biscuits. No words are really needed. I feel just a little bit humbled.

Then it's up northwards on Route 29 and across the intersection of Interstate 85, that would have led us into Montgomery, through the Tuskegee National Forest, and we make an obligatory gas stop at Natasulga. The countryside scenery here is beautiful as we also bike through areas of felled South Yellow Pine trees, which are no doubt ready to be collected and bound for the paper mills.

The roads are straight—really straight—going out into the horizon with the thick impenetrable forests now on either side of us. It almost feels a little claustrophobic with the total silence around us. Mike continues now way ahead of me but, all of a sudden, from over seventy miles per hour, in the middle of nowhere in these dense forests, we quickly come to an abrupt almost stop. Out in front is a uniformed guy standing in the middle of the road waving a flag to seriously slow us down. It looks like he means business of some sort! Half of the road has now been partitioned off for at least a good mile to create just a single lane. This means that if there were any cars coming the other way they'd have to wait quite a while to let us get through.

We're waved on, but his hand goes up and down telling us to keep at a very low speed. I wonder what's going on, but it's not long until I'm shocked to see at least one hundred uniformed prisoners, or chain gang as I think they're called, cutting and clearing grass along the roadside. A few guards with guns are watching over them. I see a few of the prisoners turn round and look at us. Being unprotected on the bike, I have an urge to ride a little faster, but Mike is keeping the speed way down. I can quite imagine one of them trying to leap onto the back of the motorbike. It's quite a sight in what feels like the middle of nowhere.

The road then mercifully opens up again, and we're off, having been the only ones to have escaped!

There is true beauty here in Alabama, passing lakes and more forests, but we're also unable to miss seeing more and more impoverished towns along the way.

Before long, we jump onto US Highway 280, which would, ultimately, take us directly into Birmingham, but this time we're going to circumnavigate the city to get to our final destination, Leeds on the northeast side and we're taking a much more interesting route. Apparently, we're going to get onto one hell of a road, which has similar traits to the infamous Tail of the Dragon back in Tennessee.

Just past Childesburg, at the junction from Harpersville, we turn right. Amazingly, and it's about time, too, we start seeing a few other bikers heading the same way. At Vincent, Mike stops his bike. He takes his helmet off. This sounds like it's going to be a serious conversation.

"Remember I told you that there's a road here now, the AL-

25N that I've been looking forward to getting on and which will take us all the way down into the valley to Leeds? It's about twenty miles, pretty bendy, but a lot of fun. I'm gonna make the most of the road and take the bends a bit aggressively." I can see him seeing my serious expression, and he continues, "I suggest we do it at our own pace and meet each other just outside Leeds. It's just straight through, and there's no way you'll get lost. Don't rush and be careful and take it at your own pace."

Words of wisdom. I take them on board. "That's fine by me. You just go and enjoy it. I'll take my time and enjoy the scenery!"

For the first time, I see Mike literally revving up and quickly accelerating away, and, although I initially try to keep up with him, it's useless, and, before long, he's cornered yet another bend and disappears out of sight. I'll enjoy the ride at my own pace, but, my God, this road is incredible, with the steepest of curves, twists, and bends that really does strongly contend with The Tail. I'm taking it easy. There's all the time in the world, but it's still pretty scary.

I finally descend down into the valley and see Mike casually parked up on the side of the road. I wonder how long he's been waiting. I see him smiling like a kid. "That was a blast. The bike did well, even with the weight of the luggage, and those curves were a fun break from all the straight roads we've been on."

It was then that I realized that he really was one excellent biker, knew totally what he was doing, and was probably feeling like he'd been finally released from a cage to go off and race round those hellish bends without me."

"Boy you just took off. I took my time and found it just a bit hairy. Pretty demanding. Thanks for waiting."

He smiles in a way that I get the feeling he knows I'm impressed. I certainly don't want to dampen his enthusiasm immediately for the route he's just done, so I refrain from asking if we're going to come back on this same road. I secretly hope not! I could personally do without it!

Reaching the outskirts of Leeds towards the end of the afternoon, we've almost reached our destination. We turn onto Rex Lake Road, where the Hampton Inn is perfectly located, just opposite the entrance into the Barber Motorsports Park and Museum. Triumph America have kindly organized our stay here, which means four nights of unadulterated comfort in air conditioned plush rooms, with no tents in sight!

We park the bikes up outside the front entrance, unload the bags onto a trolley, and wheel it to the reception desk. Mike is looking excited. "I might just bike on over to Barber to see where my guys are from the Japanese Vintage Motorcycle Club and go out for a drink with them. Are you OK with that? We can then meet early for breakfast, before biking over to the show and getting you sorted. How's that sound?"

"That's fine. As you know, I was also expecting to maybe hook up with friends tonight. Or I'll just crash." But a message is already waiting for me at reception from my good friend, Robin, of Moto Girl Café fame, who has also just arrived in town from the Carolinas. I'm also going to be spending some time with her at her booth at the Ace Corner to sign some books. Having never met in person, it would be great to at least see each other before things get started and manic tomorrow.

The message confirms what I was thinking: "Hi, Zoë. Would be great to see you tonight. We've also all been invited to a party at a friend's cafe racer workshop and home, where there'll be a BBQ, drinks, and lots of guys with cafe racers arriving to stay over for the event this weekend. Will be lots of fun. Would love you to join us. We could pick you up in the car around seven'ish. Give me a call."

Excellent. Just enough time for a quick shower and to unpack.

Robin and her husband, Scott, arrive punctually, and there are hugs all around. It had only been a few months previously that we'd initially made contact online, and Robin had initiated a great interview with me for her great online magazine, Moto Girl Café. She then suggested that, as I was endeavouring to come to the Barber Show, I also spend time with her on her stand.

What wonderful people. We head back out and arrive at an old farmstead somewhere remotely located up in the hills, otherwise known as Kiley's Garage. It's already dark, but there are lights in the trees and a lot of cool dudes are drinking beers and milling around a whole bunch of cafe racer custom bikes. Robin leads me into a massive workshop garage, where there are maybe half a dozen guys already in the middle of having started a massive project. Over the course of the weekend, they're expecting to fully complete the construction of a cafe racer bike, with parties being held here on the farm every night. Trying to absorb it all, the evening quickly disappears in this wonderful bohemian place, and, before long, the day's long journeys have caught up on us all, and we're waving goodbye and heading back. Knowing we all have a big day ahead of us tomorrow, we give each other hugs and agree on where we'll be meeting up at the show grounds.

An incredible array of things have been crammed into one day. How can that all be possible? My exhaustion is happy exhaustion, and I fall asleep smiling.

In the morning, I check in with Mike and ask how his night went. He had headed in early and called home before bed to let his family know we had arrived safely "despite Zoë's lights almost being almost punched out by a fellow biker!" as he related the tale of our diner biker encounter early yesterday.

I chuckle to myself.

5

THOUSANDS OF TWO WHEELS

Birmingham, Alabama

Already, half a mile of patient traffic; trucks, cars, lorries, camper vans and motorbikes are at a total standstill trying to climb up and round to the Barber grounds and racetrack. It's getting progressively longer, from what I can see from behind me, and it's only seven AM, with the gates and show opening in just half an hour! I'm getting frustrated, knowing I need to get to the Triumph area to unpack boxes and set up. Nothing's moving. For once, I take the lead, slowly moving the bike past Mike, who has both his feet resting on the ground, and then quickly indicate pulling over onto the side of the road. He follows suit, pulling up behind me, wondering what I'm doing.

I pull my visor up, which is already shading me from the early morning sun, and turn round in my seat to face Mike. He can see I look exasperated. "I promise you, Mike, we've got to filter through, even if you think it's illegal, and I know it's not protocol or done here, but, otherwise, we'll never get there. We're just not moving, and I can't be late!"

This isn't the first time I've seen Mike raise his eyebrows in potential disbelief on what I'm planning to do. I look seriously ahead between the three lanes of vehicles and, like a military operation, breathe deeply and start up again. I look behind to see if Mike will follow, as I'm not totally sure he will, and yet I still need him to show me the way to where we need to be. But, amazingly he follows and filters through the traffic too, and, within just a few minutes, we've reached the entry barriers. And, immediately, we're refused entry!

A lady attired with what looks like a black and white police uniform, shouts over from the entry point, "Morning, Ma'am. Where's your ID or pass? We can't give entry to anyone without them. Quick now, we're trying to get people in as quickly as possible!"

I reply imploringly, "We haven't got them yet. We're supposed to pick them up somewhere from Triumph but don't really know where. Any idea, please, where we can get them?"

"Oh, well hell, that's an easy one. Turn back round and park up by the museum, down that hill. The guys there will look after you."

Embarrassingly, after all that impatient effort to pass everyone, we're now going past the very same vehicles we went through, but in the other direction. Maybe they think we've been refused entry because we filtered. We have no other choice but to keep our heads down. But soon we're riding up to the main doors of this incredible looking place, where, already, hundreds of bikes are parked up outside the Barber Museum. I'm hoping I'll be able to visit it at some stage over the next few days.

The guys from Triumph, including Jess and Brianna, whom I've been in contact with from the Atlanta headquarters, are at a desk just within the entrance, and, after shaking hands and warmly being welcomed, we're told where their main area is in the retail section of the grounds, and both of us are given precious passes to get in and out of this enormous facility.

Before leaving, Brianna shouts out, "And, hey guys, if you're around on Monday, you'll be able to get out onto the racetrack and test it. It's because our conference is taking place here after the show."

What a shame I think. "Thanks so much. Sounds like fun, but that's the day we gotta head out back down to Florida."

"Well, don't worry. There may be opportunities to ride the circuit, anyway. Laps are done at the end of each day. I think you just need to get onto a list somewhere at the show."

We make our short way back to the gates, in an orderly fashion this time, and the same diligent guard looks at the VIP passes and gladly waves us on while shouting out, "Don't worry now, Ma'am. We know who you are now, but just keep that on you at all times. We're expecting thousands through the gates this weekend from all over the US."

I do as she says and put it round my neck and zip up my jacket tight. I can't lose it. It's my passport to this place. We ride on the smooth asphalt road up a small hill with neatly mown grass on either side and already start seeing the extent and size of this 740 acre motorsports park with its views out onto the racetrack.

The Barber Park, on the eastern fringes of Birmingham, but actually closer to Leeds, was built by George Barber and includes the famous Vintage Motorsport Museum, which is the largest motorcycle museum in the world. It's also been the site of the Indy Car Series Grand Prix of Alabama since 2010. The park opened in 2003, has a challenging 2.38 mile (3.83 km), 16 turn road course, or track, which is viewable from several naturally wooded or grass-covered banks. Many believe it to be one of the best tracks, and, hopefully, we're going to see it in action, as vintage bikes will be racing it all weekend. That'll be something to look forward to as, incredibly, I've never been to a racetrack event before.

We turn off and descend down through a small road to the back of the enormous Triumph tent, where more bikes are already parked up. This will be my main base for the next three days. People are running around and preparation is still busily underway as I walk round to introduce myself to the guys at the counter. The area is beautiful, with a massive selection of bikes on display ready for people to jump on them, comfy sofas, and, in the middle, what looks like a rocket ship.

And it's not far from the truth. It's the famous land speed racer roadster, the Triumph Castrol Rocket. It's actually a 1,000 horsepower motorcycle, with two Triumph Rocket III engines with two liquid cooled turbochargers—built like a fighter jet! The aim is to attempt to break, on the Bonneville Flats, the all-out speed record for motorcycles, which is currently set at 376.363 mph. Interestingly, it had been scheduled to do the record just a few weeks before this very show, but due to more than three inches of rain on the Flats from storms the weekend before, it's now had to be postponed until next year, in 2015.

Lucy, behind the counter and from one of the local dealers, smiles and says, "Hi Zoë. We've set you up with a small high counter and stool over there at the entrance, where you can lay out your books and chat with the folk coming in. We expect you're going to be busy. How about also parking your bike up at the front, next to the big Steve McQueen panel, so people can see what you rode when you went across this America of ours."

I thank them profusely and get myself sorted. This is exciting and like nothing I've ever done before. I'm feeling good and pretty positive that this is going to be a great few days. Mike and I lug the boxes of books from out of the truck which had transported them from the Triumph's offices in Atlanta, and we stack them on the table.

It's still quiet in the grounds, so, before the crowds start descending upon us, Mike and I take a small wander around just part of the retail zone where everyone else is setting out their stalls. Little am I to realize that this isn't all of it, just a small part of it. The event is enormous, with attractions and things happening all around the circuit from a swap meet; a famous vintage motorcycle auction; the Vintage Japanese Motorcycle Club of North America, who have an entire field showing off their own bikes; non-stop racing competitions; lots more retail areas on the other side of the track near the paddock; and the famous Ace Corner, where the cafe racers will be coming to hang out, with live music parties on every night!

People come and stay here all weekend in special RV parking and tent camping areas. It already feels like it's going to be one non-stop party.

Yes, enormous. To just get over to the Ace Corner this afternoon to be with Robin I'm going to have to take a mini-bus or softly persuade Mike to bike me over. We walk over to the edge of the grassy embankment and see the giant racetrack in front of us. Directly opposite, in the distance, is the front stretch, with the paddock area and a building we've been told to look out for. This houses a media center, the race control area, track offices, garages, and Triumph's VIP viewing area, where breakfast will be served daily if we wish to head over before the show starts. It should be the perfect place to watch some of the road racing, which starts as early as eight AM and goes on throughout the day, showcasing some of the great historic racing motorbikes. Maybe tomorrow. It seems like the main spectator areas are back over this side, otherwise known as the back stretch.

The guys over in the museum had also told us to keep an eye out for the incredible number of bizarre large sculptures like giant spiders, dragonflies, and lions, dotted around the infield part of the track and outside the museum. We walk past the Wall of Death, where the stuntmen and their bikes will be performing later, and through the retail areas of biking merchandise of every description, from hand painted helmets, souvenir t-shirts, and enough bike accessories to stock a warehouse.

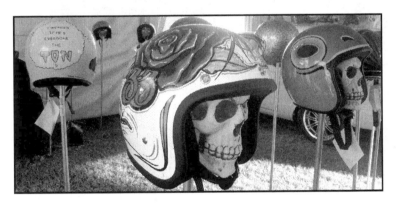

Back at Triumph the morning kicks off great, and time races away. The crowds start flooding in, and the girls at the counter are busy packing away T-shirts and gift accessories. And people are actually coming up and talking to me and buying books! There are so many inspiring stories of people and what they've done and want to do that are truly amazing. Incredibly, they're also interested in what I did. I do meet one person, though, who must have broken all records for distance. I think his name was Herb, from Kentucky, and over his biking lifetime he'd clocked up more than a million miles going back and forth across America and on other extended trips! Is that even possible? I meet many other people who've also done long distance trips like a guy called

Jim, who did 22,000 miles across America one year recently. The stories are never ending, and that's part of the joy of sharing adventures. Even if these adventures are just for a night's stop over somewhere new, they bring it all back to life again.

The girls at the counter see I've been talking a lot without much respite and that I have nothing to drink. One walks over. "Hey, remember out at the back we've a couple of coolers with drinks. Just help yourself."

I didn't see that coming and am really grateful. "Many thanks, that's great."

Before I know it, Mike's rushing back looking a little flustered and red in the face. "Hi, Zoë. I've rushed back from the Japanese Vintage field up at the top of the track and remembered we've got to get you up to Ace Corner in just a little bit. What's worse is that the lines for the buses are crazy. I'm gonna go and get my bike down here, and we can ride over. It'll only take five or ten minutes."

"That's mighty kind of you! Chauffeur service. I won't decline that!" I laugh.

We walk out of the shaded tent into the blistering heat, and I jump onto the back of the bike with Mike. We slowly filter through the crowds of people walking down the hill to the show and turn right onto the circular road sweeping up and around the course to track turn fourteen, the entrance to Ace Corner. Again, showing our passes to gain entry, we ride under a tunnel up onto a grassy area with a small display of tents around it and a big stage at the end. In the middle, on the grass, are already hundreds of bikes, the majority being beautiful handcrafted cafe racers. The music is already playing, and cool dudes are drifting around looking at what's going on and what's for sale.

I look over and see Robin is already animatedly chatting with someone on her Moto Girl area next to the stage and helping them try on a lovely leather jacket.

I walk over. "Hey Robin. How you doing? What a great time last night. Have to say I was exhausted, though, and glad of the sleep in a half decent bed, although I kept dreaming I was changing gears!"

"We, too, needed the rest before the start of these next few busy days. It's going to be exhausting. I've heard, also, that the guys we saw last night are making great progress on that bike they started building up at Kiley's. They might even try and bring it down here on Sunday!"

The feel of this area is a lot more relaxed than the frenzy down at Triumph and the retail areas. People are wandering around chatting and catching up with friends they probably haven't seen since the last show the year before. People come up to inquisitively chat and exchange stories and take copies of the books, always with a signed personal message I try to add.

After a while, Robin says, "Why don't we climb the slope over there and look out onto the racetrack. The guys from Dime City, the cafe racer outfit, are up on the stage, and I know Breeann wanted to interview us about how we got it all together. Let's go and see, but not before catching a beer on the way!"

The slope is pretty steep, and I almost stumble up it and slide back down on it on my bum, but, once there, I can now start to understand why they say Ace Corner has one of the best vantage points of the track. Just below us, the bikes are now racing past creating massive noise, which means trying to speak in any way coherently into the microphone is nigh on impossible. We decide to abandon that one and try something later down on the other stage.

After just a few hours, Mike's back again to pick me up, but not before we've all agreed to meet for dinner later on. It's Mike this time who says he knows a very decent place which serves good steaks and beers. We all smile and nod with that suggestion.

We ride back down the hill, and by now every inch of the grass verges on either side of the road has every imaginable kind of bike parked up and squeezed in. There must be thousands, and the majority of these people will be staying on the grounds camping. Party on!

By the end of the day, with people slowly leaving, I go over to the girls to thank them and put the remaining books back in the boxes and hide them under a table until tomorrow.

My bike had done well, being a bit of a show piece all day, with people wanting photos taken of it with me, them, and the book! Again, something I'm still trying to take in. What? Just little old me!

Walking over to me, holding my helmet, Mike says, "I was thinking we'll take the long route round the park before leaving tonight so we can ride up and around behind the paddock up at the top, figure out where the hospitality area is in case we want breakfast tomorrow, and get another view of this place."

We head out round the beautiful tree lined road, and, looking out over the track, I spot the massive steel spider. The traffic has dissipated to almost nothing, and, within fifteen minutes, we're back at the comfy luxury of the hotel.

Mike looks seriously at me. "I know you were really nervous about today and what to expect and how people would treat you. But how do you feel now about how the day went?"

I reply immediately, without the slightest hesitation, "Beyond my wildest expectations. The generous nature of everyone and the openness of everyone wanting to exchange stories was amazing. And I think I probably signed quite a few books to go with that. I'm over the moon. I feel like I have to pinch myself that I'm not dreaming."

Later that evening, Robin, Scott, Mike, and myself are sitting at the bar at the well-known Logan's Roadhouse Bar and Grill drinking chilled beers, and eating peanuts, chucking their shells on the floor, which is a well-known and totally accepted practice here. Looking over our shoulders and seeing enormous juicy steaks and French fries being served up to the neighbouring tables, we quickly race to grab the menu cards to order exactly the same.

6

Alabama Blues

Gluttons for punishment, we, the two intrepid bikers, are once again up at the crack of dawn. We enter the Barber grounds, this time without any problem of massive back-ups, as most of the camper vans and trucks arrived yesterday to set up. True to her word, the guard at the gates recognises us, or our badges now firmly on display around our necks, and happily waves us through.

It's Saturday. It's going to be, by far, the busiest day, and I start getting myself psyched up as I see the first swarms of people walking down the hill to the tent. Two hours in, my voice is rasping and going almost dry, having spoken with so many people, but the feeling is wonderful and priceless.

Mike approaches me with a couple of bottles of water and pulls me away. "Hey, Zoë, pace yourself. Here!" giving me one of the bottles, "Let's go and sit and rest under that tree for ten minutes and watch what's racing around the track."

I look over to the lovely girls at the desk, who nod and put their thumbs up that they'll keep an eye out if I need to come back. We sit down on the grassy bank under the tree and look out to the majestic circuit, with the sounds of loud engines echoing into the distance.

"So, Zoë, it's going good, but you're looking like you're in deep thought mode. I know what it is. You're already thinking about tonight and how you're going to try and get over to Bessemer and meet Melissa. I warn you, that place is out in the sticks, more than twenty miles south of Birmingham and in a really poor, run-down community. Not a place for a girl to go to by herself on a bike in the dark, and especially if she doesn't know the place!"

"I have to. This opportunity is too important, and, anyway, I feel like I already know her, as we've talked so much by email. And as you know, also being a lover of music, one of the main reasons for coming to the South was to discover some of the remaining blues music joints."

I sit back against the tree and close my eyes, and the warmth and distant humming of the bikes puts me almost in a trance-like state as I'm transported back just three months ago, when the idea of this trip over to America was being brought to life.

As usual, I was scrimping and saving to find the money to even pay for the flight, and I'd thought that maybe an extra opportunity while in Birmingham would be to maybe suss out a music night venue where I could possibly go to sign some books as it was Barber week. Or at the very least, and a bit of a romantic dream fantasy, to just hang out in an underground little known smoky blues joint, sitting in a corner with cool dudes, while being blown away by the feel of the very best in true Deep South music—too good to miss. I had put the feelers out, maybe initially out of pure curiosity. Again, I found out how the Internet is able to bring people together. Over the summer, I trawl and pull up something I feel may be able to help— the *American Blues Scene Magazine*. If these guys didn't know, then I'd have problems. Matt Marshall's the guy I finally made contact with. I explained what I'd been thinking, that it would be great to find a special place that resonates with the soul of true blues music and to ideally visit it with some of my friends from the show.

The reply back was miraculous. "Yes, Alabama has some really good talent in the blues arena, but there is just one historic important music venue and experience—a true Alabama treasure. I'd like to introduce you to Melissa and Gip. Gip runs "Gip's Place", one of the last remaining, most cherished and longstanding juke joints in the country; a place where people have been coming to hear blues for fifty years. It really should be a national landmark. The best part? It's in Birmingham; Bessemer to be exact. But I am already worried there may be some big potential issues, basically noise, with bikes coming to this location."

"Anyway, Melissa works with Gip to help oversee many day-to-day activities. As fate would have it, her husband also works at the largest motorcycle dealership in the state and is involved with the Vintage Bike Fest. And she's very excited about the potential possibilities I've mentioned to her about your visit."

I had never heard of the term juke joint and was fascinated to know more. I quickly did a bit of research and realized that there are probably no more than a handful of these original places still in existence across America. Historically, close to the farms, they were the places slaves could go to and play some form of music when they were not working, which was usually just a Sunday. They were a place to dream and play from the depth of their hearts.

That very same evening, I received a wonderful heartfelt message: "Hi, it's Melissa here. I've thought this through. Gip's place is small, primitive, peaceful, and very magical to the human spirit. Mr. Gip, honestly, has done more for the racial divide that has plagued the South, than any large non-profit group. Of course, that is my opinion.

"Gip's mantra of "No White, no Black, just Blues" is just about the synopsis of his life. Now his location is nestled deep in a completely Black, poor neighbourhood. This, to me and scores of fans from around the world, adds to the charm of the place. We do our thing every Saturday night. A different blues band each week comes to visit. Our policy is open door, ten dollar "donations" at the gate, and people bring in whatever they wish to eat or drink. We start each night with prayer, and we end at midnight. It has a magical atmosphere, with Christmas lights and Mardi Gras beads dangling from the ceiling. All around the walls are old authentic posters of the likes of Robert Johnson and Muddy Waters. We have no telephone number, so people just have to turn up.

"But I have to be honest about you possibly coming with bikes and a lot of people. It's this: Last Spring, Mr. Gip was nearly put into extinction by the very city he loves and has been in for more than seventy years. Had it not been for social media, a worldwide fan base, and people like Matt Marshall from *American Blues Scene*, Mr. Gipson would not be in this conversation. So...the fact that hundreds of motorcycles in his neighbourhood, cranking up at midnight...really worries me. Let me say, though...Mr. Gipson would love it. He loves motorcycles of any kind, and we'll be bringing him to the Vintage Fest. The iconic Mr. Gip is living history, one of a kind, and once he's gone this will be the end of the historic juke joints. Let me know what you think."

I was truly fascinated by what Melissa has just opened up to tell me, and I was curious to find out more about the authenticity and fame of Mr. Gip. What I dig up leaves me speechless.

Henry Gipson grew up in the tiny place of Uniontown, Alabama, just west of Selma, more than ninety years ago. He then moved to Bessemer and worked at the Pullman Railcar Company for twenty-five years, then began working for a funeral home, digging graves. He owns his own cemetery fifteen miles west of Birmingham and still digs the graves himself.

But it wasn't until I pulled up a short clip of an old man with a guitar in his hands, talking about his life with that soft deep almost indecipherable Southern accent, that I was profoundly moved.

This is what he recounts: "Here down in Hueytown me and a person called Joe Lucas started playing together and went down the mines. We used to go down there and play. We had been playing for three weeks and people liked it. At that time a lot of Klan members were running around with their hoods on and I went down to Hueytown one evening to play for a man called AC Shaw and all of a sudden I was back on the floor. They broke my guitar up, my hand was knobbed up. My hand has been broke, steel pins coming out. I can't spread my fingers no more. I have to crowd my fingers now, when I used to spread my hands out to play. I couldn't after that. I had to learn about three years later how to use my hand.

"Music and blues don't care no color. When I started, it got so crowded people would come and couldn't get through the door. People would stop in the road just to listen to see what's happening. Next thing I knew, had to have a permit. Never had hours for closing down, no hours to start. If anybody wants to come they went down to the police station and say, "We're trying to get to Mr. Gip's Place." The Chief will get in the car and lead them here. It's just love and it shocks me a lot of times. Music represents life. It burns within a person to see what he could be. And that's why I love blues because blues deals with a story to tell you."

And since 1952, Mr. Gip Gipson has opened the backyard of his home at 3101 Avenue C, where great blues musicians have gathered and where blues parties happen every Saturday night. It truly is one of the most cherished and longstanding authentic juke joints in America.

But not loved by all! Just a year before, in 2013, the police raided it and shut it down, due to what some thought was too much music. According to the Bessemer Police Department, the reason for the raid was he was running an illegal business. "The establishment has caused quite a bit of problems for the neighbours of Mr. Gipson. Many are elderly. We have received multiple calls from homeowners over the last several months, who say loud music from Gip's Place has inhibited their sleep!"

Melissa and I continued communicating throughout the summer, but, with all the effort we put in, the likelihood of bringing a biking party to the venue seemed less and less likely, but more and more likely that, without a doubt, I will do everything I possibly could to go and meet Melissa and Mr. Gip and experience something I felt would be very, very special.

I'm prodded in the arm by Mike and brought back to reality. "Looks like you were miles away. Got any further in thinking how you're getting to Bessemer?"

Stretching my arms over my head, I reply, "I'll find a way. Maybe some of the guys at Ace, when I see them later, will fancy going, and we could jump into one of their cars and drive over."

Mike replies kindly, but honestly, "I'd have tried biking us there, but the place is pretty remote and I've promised my ADVRider friends, who are camping out nearby, that tonight I would drop by, hang out at the camp fire with them, and have a beer or two, but you're also welcome to join us."

I smile, appreciating his openness, "It's not a problem. I'll find a way."

We walk back to the tent and have another frenetic few hours mingling and chatting with everyone. Towards the end of the afternoon, leaving the bike at the Triumph tent, I jump on one of the shuttle buses and head back over to Ace Corner to see who's around. I'm chatting animatedly with Robin, when Mark and Steve—the guys setting up the new Ace Cafe USA, in Orlando—wander over with a handful of friends and ask exactly what I want to hear.

Mark smiles. "So, hey, girls. What are we all doing tonight?"

Robin smiles back. "Well, Scott and I are going back up to Riley's later, so we've got plans."

Then I answer, with what hopefully sounds laid back, "Me? Well I'm trying to find a way to get to a place called Bessemer to go and check out this incredible juke joint." I go on to explain what it's all about and everyone definitely seems interested.

"That sounds real cool. I'd like to check it out, too," continues Mark. "Let's get a crew of people to head down there. All the cars are parked around here, so we can leave immediately after the show finishes and after we've heard a bit of the live music here on the stage. There's a couple of local people with us, and we can follow them in the cars. Makes sense."

A blond girl in the crowd chirps up with a beautiful Southern accent, "Yea. That's a mighty fun place. I was there just a few weeks ago with friends. It was jumping. I'll definitely take my car, as I need to get back to Birmingham afterwards. You guys can just follow me, as that place is pretty tough to find."

Great. That was easier than I'd expected. I text Mike that I'll be leaving the bike at the grounds and that I can simply pillion back with him tomorrow morning to the show. All I need do now is keep a close eye on this group so I don't lose them and loose my ride.

The sun starts to go down, and very quickly it's dark, with people wandering with beers in their hands to the stage blasting with live rock 'n' roll music. Soon everyone seems to be on the move again, with bikes being started up and leaving, no doubt going on to some other party.

I turn from the stage and look around me. Panic sets in. Where have Mark and the group gone to? All of a sudden it feels like they've disappeared, and I'm left all on my own. This can't be possible. I run across the grass to the small entrance and, incredibly, see the blond Southern belle, who looks like she's also just about to leave.

I run up to her without even knowing her name. "Hey, Hi, it's Zoë. We spoke earlier. Are you still heading to Mr. Gips? Is there anyway I could go with you? I seem to have lost everyone."

"Hey, good to see you again, too. I'm Savannah and, yea, I'm definitely going, but same as you, they all seem to have disappeared. Although I did say I'd meet my friends up in the car park field, up and over the hill. They were going to follow me over there. But it's quite a walk up there. We'd better hurry or they may have already left."

I agree. "OK, I'm with you. I guess we'd better get going."

We rush out from Ace Corner and quickly try to see if there are still any buses running that we can catch—nothing. Then, from the corner of my eye, parked up in the dark is a small Mule ATV with someone in the driver's seat. We're maybe lucking out.

I walk over and put my "pleading hat" on and panicky English accent, which will hopefully bring a little sympathy. "Hi there. Is there any way you could take us up the hill to where we've parked the car? Our friends are waiting for us up there, and we're afraid they're going to leave and head out before we get there. We're all supposed to be following each other to the other side of Birmingham."

The guy smiles and says, "Sure. I was headed up that way, anyway. Hop in but I have to say..."

Without waiting for the guy to finish what he's trying to tell us, Savannah literally jumps into the open rear area of the Mule truck, which quickly, without notice, reverses backwards, opening the latched back panel and rudely drops Savannah out into the muddy ground.

I run up to her. "Oh my God, are you OK?"

"Scary. My jeans are now a bit muddy, but it could have been a lot worse. My hair could have got destroyed!"

The guy jumps out and runs round to us. "I was gonna add that you need to hop in at the front with me. The back latch doesn't work, and I was simply just going to reverse so you could jump in. Sorry."

We arrive in the dark field and, without a torch, miraculously and quickly find the car among the hundreds of others, thanks mainly to the light from the starry sky and full moon. Savannah looks around and immediately smiles, recognising her friends waiting patiently in their car. "They're still here because I'm pretty much the only one who knows, more or less, how to get there, being local to Birmingham. I wish the other guys who've already left the best of luck 'cos it's definitely not going to be that easy, even with their GPS! Let's go, and the other two cars can follow us."

This will be a journey of one hundred percent trust. I don't know the girl from Adam, I don't know where we're going, and it's totally dark and impossible to know if we're even going in the right direction. I'm somehow convincing myself it'll be fine. But my heart is uncontrollably palpitating just slightly.

To be truthful, there had only been one other major occasion in my life that I can remember going on a long trip in a car to a place I didn't know, oh, yes, and in the dark with a total stranger. I was young and naive. Just twenty-one years old, and I was flying over from Paris to Detroit on my own to incredibly see and convince the Big Three—Ford, General Motors, and Chrysler—to go to the other side of the world and attend the first automotive show in Shanghai, China, the following year—"Automotive China." Being typically French, my boss was prioritizing his summer holiday to the Cote d'Azur, so he delegated the job to me, as I was the only person who spoke English. I was going to meet their VPs of International Business in their Detroit factories. It was quite a challenge, as I didn't really know one end of a car from another and hadn't really read up too much about importing cars to China, which, at that stage, only had Russian black limos for government officials and a few weather-beaten Japanese taxis. There were, literally, no cars at that stage in the mid '80s, just millions of bicycles, which I would encounter and experience myself.

Anyway, I'm side tracking. Flying over, I started chatting with a lovely lady who told me she lived just outside Detroit and that we should maybe meet up while I was in her city. She did warn me, though, to not walk out on my own and to be very careful, as it was considered a very dangerous place. I naively agreed, and, the next day, I was waiting for her in the hotel lobby to pick me up and show me around. She didn't arrive, but a big, bearded guy did. She hadn't mentioned that! He sweetly told me that he was her boyfriend and we'd drive over to their home close to the lakes, which was only thirty or forty miles away. And, you know what? I said yes, but the ride over wasn't a comfortable one, as I was never a hundred percent sure where we were going and who he was. There were no cell phones then to double check. Luckily, it all worked out, and we had a great time, but, boy, I was glad to see her smiling face waving from their house when we arrived!

But the cheery face of Savannah and her magic words of being a "local to Birmingham" reassures me totally. No chance of getting lost I hope, or going somewhere else. We both get into her massive, black-windowed Lincoln, I sink into the leather seat, and Savannah immediately smiles wickedly and gets the night going by turning up the volume to the local music station while tapping a hand on the wheel and smoking a cigarette with the other. I smile with her and already feel like I've been sucked into some form of eccentric Southern hospitality.

We soon hit the highway, with Savannah continuously looking in her rear view mirror and braking from time to time. It soon looks like she may have put her foot down a bit too hard and speeded away from the other cars. She casually says, "They'll be alright. One of them has GPS, and the others have Georgia, who also knows the place. But it's probably not a place to stop and ask for directions, so they'd better stay together and in the car. We all know that the surest way to get to Gip's Place is to go with somebody who's been there before and knows how to find it 'cos it sure ain't easy to find!"

Before long, we're slowly driving up and down the same roads through a quiet but poor looking area. I'm feeling already that coming on a bike on my own, in the dark, would have been a nightmare.

"I know it's around here somewhere. We're real close. You'd never believe it, but it just looks like a normal house. It's all the trucks that'll be parked up outside that will give it away."

And then, there it is. There are people getting out of their trucks and walking down a narrow pathway, through a gate, to a small, white wooden panelled, one storey house.

Savannah walks to the back of the car. "Looks like we're the first of the gang here. I've still got a box of beers in the back here, which we can pull out.

So, with that, and carrying two or three bottles of beer each, we also walk down to Mr. Gip's Place. Nothing more than a very small fenced garden, or back yard, greets us with a few rickety plastic chairs and tables. We walk through what looks like a back door to the house, where we're greeted and handed Mardi Gras beaded necklaces, which are wrapped around our necks. We enter a darkly lit room with no more than ten or fifteen small tables tightly packed together, a few rustic benches lining the walls, and a small but well lit and equipped stage at the front. And, yes, all around the walls are pictures and posters of blues legends.

The description from what I've read and imagined is incredibly accurate, with small Christmas lights sparkling and hanging from everywhere. A few local people are already seated along the walls, quietly waiting for the evening to begin and no doubt curious to see the sort of "out-of-towners" the evening will bring. One guy particularly stands out and is totally dapper, wearing a white trilby hat, orange flared trousers, and matching orange shirt, with shiny white and gold dance shoes. He already looks ready to get up and dance.

We walk to a small round table at the front, near the dance floor and stage, put all the bottles of beer onto it, and sit down. Some musicians are already warming up, testing the sound system while strumming a few chords.

I look around, soaking up the atmosphere. "Savannah. Are you OK if I go and find Melissa, who I've told you about?"

"Sure, and I'll keep an eye out for the guys." She takes out a bottle opener from her handbag and, expertly opening a beer, she laughs, "But if they're not here soon, there'll be no room inside, and they'll be looking in from the window outside in the garden!"

I finally spot Melissa chatting with people outside in the garden.

"Hey, Melissa. Finally we meet. It's Zoë, and I've actually managed to get here with a few friends and without the bikes!"

She smiles and gives me a big hug. "Welcome. So glad you're here. It's gonna be a good one. Mr. Gip is going to play tonight, and we have the amazing Debbie Bond and the TruDats Band. You'll no doubt see him later, as he tries to greet all his guests and will go over the house rules with those he doesn't know—no drugs, no profanity, and no baggy pants. And you'll see every night we start with a prayer."

By the time I get back to our seats, everyone has arrived and squeezed in next to us. The room is packed. There's a feeling of magic here, and I reckon we're in for a treat. The lights dim even further, and someone arrives on the stage. Everything goes quiet. Evening prayers are said, and then, immediately, the first band starts up. I see Mr. Gip, finally, from the corner of my eye, dressed smartly in a black suit, T-shirt, and black Stetson hat angled to one side, walking onto the dance floor and immediately up to Savannah, pulling her from her chair to start dancing with her! Fantastic! Then, it's my turn. He firmly takes me by the hand and literally swings me around the floor. Everyone's clapping and cheering. It looks like he's loving life with all these new people in his home. The warm up band finally closes its set, and I see Melissa and Mr. Gip walk onto the stage.

They thank everyone for coming tonight, and then I have to do a double take in what I hear, "And we'd specially like to thank tonight our friends from Barber with Zoë. Come on up onto the stage!"

What? Us! Mark, Steve, Savannah, and I get up, a little embarrassed, and climb onto the stage. I wasn't expecting that. We chat a bit about what we're all doing here in Birmingham, and then more great music starts up again. The dance floor seems to take on its own life, shaking with everyone dancing on it, including the dapper orange-suited gentleman, who is in his element, asking every woman he sees to dance with him.

Then Mr. Gip, carrying his guitar, returns to the stage and starts singing and playing in such a deep, emotional way. The sound of this real blues music, with all its own heartfelt and life experienced lyrics and gritty chords, resonates through everybody. Then he changes tempo, and everyone goes crazy and jumps up to dance again.

The bands and wonderful music continue all night. The midnight curfew for playing the music arrives only too soon, and we all quietly and respectfully leave the sleeping neighbourhood. But it doesn't stop Savannah and me from singing at the top of our voices all the way back to Birmingham!

7

CHRISTMAS TREE OF BIKES

Birmingham, Alabama

I'm feeling just a little bit jaded and worse for wear from the previous evening. I hang on tightly to the back of the bike as it swerves quickly round the bends up to the Barber racetrack. Mike expertly pulls to a halt on the grass next to my own bike outside the Triumph tent, and I delicately get off. I bend down and look into the rear view mirror. Although my eyes look a bit red, I reassure myself that I look just fine, but pull the baseball hat down just slightly.

The girls smile and wave over to me, the music is already pelting out from the speakers and the hum of the bikes are buzzing round and round the track, as another day begins, with the crowds arriving on this last day.

Towards the end of the morning, we've incredibly sold most of the books, and I see a window of opportunity too good to miss. Mike is sitting on a stool, flipping through a bike magazine. "Hey, Mike. I'm gonna walk down to the museum and finally take a quick wander inside and see what everyone's been talking about."

"Yea," looking up, "you'd better. There won't be another chance." He looks at his watch. "While we're here we should also bike over to the other side of the racetrack at lunchtime and try and get a view from the terraces up by the hospitality suites. We've got our VIP badges so it shouldn't be a problem getting in. I've never been up there before, but people have told me that's the place for the best views of the track. It looks right down on the starting line and should be great photo opportunity for my magazine photos."

"Sounds like a plan, Stan. See you in a bit."

I walk slowly back up the hill to retain my energy, now being the hottest part of the day, and back down on the other side to the Barber Museum. From the outside, with its immaculately kept green lawns, the modern frontage is almost entirely glass clad reaching up five storeys. During the numerous conversations I've had with people over the last few days, they all said it's a great place to see the history of motorcycles from all around the world and is, apparently, the best collection of bikes anywhere in the world."

Walking inside, escaping the heat, with hardly another person in sight, I see an impressive spiral walkway twisting up through the middle of the building. I start strolling up and around it. I'm immediately dumb struck to see the place is just chock-a-block with motorcycles being displayed in every conceivable and imaginable space. Rows of bikes are suspended and hanging from walls, to layers and layers displayed closely packed one on top of the other through the five floors, and, apparently, a lot aren't even on display.

Yes, it's a fact, with bikes spanning over a hundred years of production, this is home to the world's best and largest motorcycle collection, with over 1,350 vintage and modern little beauties from two hundred manufacturers and twenty countries. I'm pretty convinced this must be true, as I lean over the banisters from the fifth floor and look down the dizzying height to the hundreds of bikes on display, some proudly positioned on stands overlooking the racetrack. And there are obviously all sorts from Harley-Davidson, Honda, Triumph, and Indian, as well as names I've, embarrassingly, never heard of like Showa, DSK, and Cagiva. I even see an old bike, which was motored by steam! Looking down to the ground floor, there's even an area where live renovation demonstrations are held in one of the workshop areas. One of the central features is truly amazing. Going up through all five floors, almost reaching the roof, can only be described as a Christmas tree shape of hundreds of layered bikes. In fact, the interior structure of the place is a little reminiscent to the Guggenheim Museum in Bilbao, Spain.

This spectacular showpiece of a museum was founded less than twenty years ago by a Birmingham native, George Barber, who successfully raced, with more than sixty wins, and kept Porches in the 1960s. He started collecting and restoring classic sports cars and, in 1989, started doing the same with motorcycles. Barber quickly recognised there wasn't a place which represented and showed the global history of motorcycles, so he quickly set up the first museum in 1995, which then moved to the current grounds here in 2003. Some of these bikes are so rare and collectible that the museum was ranked as being the greatest lender to exhibitions in New York, Chicago, and Bilbao.

It's all quite mesmerizing, but I also know time isn't in my favour and that I need to quickly head back, but this has been quite an experience. I walk out of the cool air conditioned building and back into the sweltering Alabama heat. And this is Autumn!

Mike is still patiently seated on the stool with what looks like a pile of thumbed through magazines on the table. He immediately jumps up when he sees me. "Hey. How did it go? Were you impressed?"

"Absolutely! Not that I know a lot about bikes, but the museum was beautiful, and the number and diversity on display were spectacular."

"Yea. I know. Some guys spend hours and hours in there and then have to go back again. We had quite a few people come and get the book and say they'd come back later to see if they can have a chat with you. And guess who appeared out of the blue?"

That answer I couldn't guess.

"It was those three guys, you know, who we met at Dee's over in Vernon the other day and who almost created a scene!"

"Oh, that's too bad," I say a little disappointed. "Maybe we'll see them again later?"

"That's right. I told them to pop by after lunch. And, hey, it's about that time of the day. Shall we bike over to the other side of the racetrack and see what's happening?"

So, not for the first time today, I jump back onto Mike's bike, and we ride on over to the paddock area, where all races start, and down to the Race Control Building. Thankfully, showing our precious badges, we easily gain access and park the bikes right outside the paddock area, where hundreds of guys and bikes are slowly riding or pushing their race bikes in and out of the building, getting ready to go out and race. It's quite a spectacle and theatrical hive of activity. Showing our special badges to gain access, we press the elevator button and go up to the outside viewing deck looking out onto the track. I smile. I can see Mike is in his element, enthusiastically leaning over the wall and taking pictures below him of the riders getting ready to start racing.

Like a kid in a candy store, he looks around smiling. "Hey! Isn't this awesome. I've never seen the racetrack from this height or vantage point before. We're really lucky."

"I agree. It's really good. I've also got some other good news finalized this morning, when I picked up my phone messages leaving the museum. Rick and Gary, from Rok Straps, e-mailed and confirmed that I can definitely be with them for a few hours each day at AIMExpo. They seemed pretty thrilled about it all. I guess it helps if one of them is a chilled out Aussie. So that's all sorted."

"Great news. That show is pretty new but getting real important. But you'll see it's very different from here!"

With that, we leave the paddock, with all its hustle and bustle, and bike back to the Retail Zone on the other side, via the Ace Corner to say our farewells to Robin. She walks up smiling. "Sounds like you guys had a great time over at the music joint last night. Heard the stories!" And, with that, I see Mark, from Ace, also walking towards us.

"Quite a night! Glad we did it. We're out of here today, but, no doubt, we'll be bumping into each other in Orlando for the show. We've got a special press event being held at the new Ace venue in the downtown district. Make sure that you and Mike get to it. It should be interesting because no building or dismantling has started yet on the site, so you'll see what the famous old music joint originally looked like. And there's also breakfast there, on us!" With that, he quickly disappears, not for the first time, into the crowds.

Robin and I give each other one last hug, and then we head back to the Triumph area for one last time. I spend another few precious hours chatting with people, getting pictures taken of them next to the Bonneville, and enjoy lots of laughter hearing different people's own stories and adventures, and the show is coming to a close.

Both bikes are now parked up outside the tent, close to the British Customs demo area. Mike looks around like he's looking for something. "I wonder if there's anyone with tools here. I don't have a wrench big enough to loosen the rear axle."

I smile, thinking that if there was any place with tools, this would have to be it!

He continues, "I'd like to check and maybe tighten the chains and get the tyres topped off before heading back on the road tomorrow." And, with that, he kneels down conscientiously on the grass, seriously looking under his bike, why I've no idea, and pulling the chain up and down.

While he's doing that, I walk round and see the guys at the Californian outfit, British Customs, doing exactly that—bikes on a ramp, checking tyres and stuff. I walk up to one of them and explain the situation. A cool guy named Matt smiles and points to their ramp. "Sure, no problem. We're doing a few for other guys at the moment. Wheel the bikes round and we can check them."

How good is that! Soon I'm convinced that I now definitely want one of their cafe racer seats, ideally the brown leather, and have one stowed away with me for my bike back home!

With both bikes checked over, we walk over and hug the Triumph girls goodbye, thanking them profusely for having helped us have such a great time. The promotional banner is rolled up again and tied back down on the back of my seat.

Before Mike starts up, he quickly mentions, "Oh, yes. There's just one last thing I need to do before leaving. I've got to go back to the Vintage Japanese Motorcycle Club's bike field and say farewell to the VJMC guys and quickly discuss my plans with them for AIMExpo. I think they're also doing some drinks. Oh, yes, and there's also something there that you've just got to check out! It might be some kind of compensation for us not getting out onto the racetrack. I did try but it was all booked up."

We enter the field on the top of the hill and park up where Mike needs to see his guys, and I wander around looking at the bike exhibits. It's there that I see it. On display is what must be the longest, biggest bike I've ever seen. And when I say long, I mean long! It's got to be about sixteen or twenty feet long, but with only two seats for the rider and a pillion. This bizarre machine is called "Roaddog"!

I curiously walk up to the sign next to it. In 1965, William "Wild Bill' Gelbke built Roaddog to become the world's largest motorcycle. This ginormous bike is seventeen feet long, weighs 3,280 lbs, has a wheelbase of 126 inches, with a twenty-five miles per gallon fuel consumption, and can do 125 miles with a five gallon tank. Its engine is enormous—a four-cylinder Chevy with automatic transmission. Wild Bill then toured the US, riding more than 20,000 miles and reaching speeds of more than ninety miles per hour on it!

Wild Bill was something of a legend. His mother told stories of his childhood exploits, like his attempt to outfit a baby pram with a washing machine motor! Gelbke was actually a qualified engineer for McDonnell Douglas and Hughes Aircraft, but "Wild Bill" longed for excitement, so he opened up a bike shop and started designing motorcycles. Roaddog was one of his biggest endeavours.

It also seems that Gelbke was quite a character and free spirit. They say he'd spontaneously jump on Roaddog from his home in Chicago and ride to Texas or Oklahoma just for a good steak or beer! His engineering and pioneering achievements were incredible, with the bike clocking up major firsts: twin headlights, automatic transmission with reverse, four hydraulic stands to keep it upright when parked, and disc brakes front and rear from a Corvette.

Apparently, because of its size and unusual drive characteristics, there were only a few people who were ever able to ride it. One of the comments on its handling characteristics was, "You have to be an Olympic weightlifter to move the bars while standing still; once moving, you have to be an Olympic weightlifter to move the bars!"

There's just one more thing to do. I look around. The field's pretty empty now, with most people now drinking beers inside the tent. I walk up to Roaddog's single rider's black leather-fringed and studded seat and put a leg over and sit down. My God! The handlebars are massive, and the wheels have got to be the size of truck wheels. It feels like something out of a sci-fi movie. Out of nowhere, a friendly, smiling guy unexpectedly walks up to me and also reads the panel.

"Hey! You wanna photo taken? It's one hell of a bike. The guys over there told me it was for sale. I wonder who the hell would buy it!"

Later that evening, Mike and I have biked over to Ruby Tuesday, just up the road from where we ate the other night and just north of Interstate 20, for a Southern crab cake dinner.

We lift the bottles of iced beer from the table and click them together.

"Cheers! As they say in the UK!" smiles Mike.

"Cheers and thanks for everything. It's been fun and a pretty unique experience."

"Yea. We've packed in quite a bit over the last few days. So, tomorrow, and obviously early, we've got an interesting route back. We're heading through Georgia and stopping over at a friend's in Valdosta, close to the Georgia and Florida border. When we get back to Lake Wales the day after, you're gonna have a few days free before we hit the next event in Orlando. Have you made any plans or got any ideas on what you want to do?"

"Yes. I'm really looking forward to it. I've been thinking I'm going to ride down further south and try and get some sea air and put my feet in the sand, but I'm looking for somewhere quiet and pretty. I'm tempted to head to the keys south of St.

Petersburg. Apparently, reading up about it back in London, the St. Pete Beach area is supposed to be really nice, quiet, and with great stretches of beach. I just need to find a half-decent place to stay for a few nights, right on the beach."

Mike looks shocked and exclaims, "Oh boy! Don't even go close to St. Petersburg! It gets real congested, getting through it will take forever, and I think your idea of tranquillity certainly won't be the case over at St. Pete. I've got a much better idea and a much better kept secret, which is what I know you'll like better. Where I'm thinking, the beaches should be pretty empty and pristine at this time of year, and the shoreline drive on that stretch of the keys is great."

This is sounding good and just up my street in how he's describing the place.

He puts his bottle of beer down and pulls out a pen from his shirt pocket and starts drawing a basic road map on his paper serviette. "Take a look. Better still, it's not far from where we live, easy to get to along small, pretty country roads, and you'll definitely have no major traffic congestion to contend with. It's a place called Longboat Key, which you'll need to cross over a long bridge to get to, and it's just up from Sarasota. I promise you. That's the place to go to, and you're sure to find lots of small, quaint places to stay right on the beach."

He's talking as a true local of the area, and it sounds exactly where I want to head to. "That sounds perfect. Sarasota."

"Yea, it's known in Florida as our arts and cultural center, with the Sarasota Opera and Ringling Museum, among other things. A pretty place to go and see if you get the time."

So with those seeds of inspiration sown on where to go and explore when we get back to Florida, we drink up our beers and head back to the hotel to get ourselves and the bikes packed up and ready to hit Georgia tomorrow.

8

RAINY NIGHT IN GEORGIA

Leeds, Alabama to Valdosta, Georgia

350 miles

By the time we're wheeling the bikes round to the front of the hotel to load them with all our travelling paraphernalia, at least twenty like-minded people have done the same, with a few curious "normal' hotel guests standing close by looking inquisitively at what all the fuss is about. There are bikes of all descriptions, from beautiful vintage Ducatis and Triumphs to large, heavy duty adventure bikes. Everyone has the same mission. To check the bikes over, set their sat-nav or look over the maps again, and safely get them packed for the next road trip, wherever that takes them.

For some strange reason, although I had nothing more than what we'd brought, the bike looks surprisingly more heavily charged than when it had arrived. I'm obviously not a good "re-packer" in squeezing stuff into small spaces. I pull the straps down tight to secure the bag and the enormous banner, encased in its long round cylinder, on top. I think we're ready.

I look up at the Alabama early morning sky, and, although cloudy, it's warm, which makes me smile, feeling like it's a good day for getting back on the road. I wheel the empty trolley back into the hotel lobby and walk out, strapping my helmet on. Mike is fastening his and getting on.

There is just one question I nervously want to ask him before he starts up, so I'm prepared for the answer. "Are you intending to take the AL25 southwards, the same way we arrived?"

Mike smiles. "Yea I know. I had fun biking round those twenty miles of bends, and it wouldn't take much to tempt me to get back on it, but, as I've already reassured you, you don't need to worry! We're gonna head instead east out of Leeds, so no knees on the ground first thing in the morning. 'though maybe later!"

He puts his thumb up, raises his eyebrows, and nods questioning if I'm ready to go: "Are you ready to follow your Road Dog today?"

I smile and nod back. Both bikes start up. We cross the quiet junction, turn right, and before soon have left the main highway onto a much smaller country road. I look in my rear view mirror and see the cylinder behind me is a bit lopsided. I take my left hand carefully off the handlebar and feel behind me that the luggage is tightly secured down. It feels OK. The last thing I want to do is suddenly have to stop in the road and run back to collect my stuff, which, hopefully, won't have been run over.

But, this morning, the small roads we're on leaving Leeds are quiet, with only the cows contently mooing in the fields. That's what I like. There's no need to stop for breakfast as we've already grabbed some at the hotel, and, besides stopping for gas along the way, we reckon we should probably reach Georgia in just a couple hours. Last night Mike had pencilled over the map, calculating it was probably only about a hundred and twenty miles cross country to the state line.

Just a few miles farther on the quiet roads, we find and get onto Interstate 20 East, to bring us back to reality on a Monday morning that some people have to go to work. But, almost instantly, we leave it at Pell City, down along Route 34, to then get us southbound onto Route 77 to the Georgia border. These are now real small roads and so pretty, with the leaves just starting to change colour.

No sooner have I thought all is well, and admiring a quaint little water mill we're passing, that I see Mike looking behind his shoulder, then down to his map on the tank bag, then quickly signalling right to park up on the side of the road. I somehow feel we may be on the wrong road or going in the wrong direction.

Mike turns his engine off. "I think I've turned too soon. I'm a bit confused. I did see a boat dealership just down the hill by the mill. We should just go and ask the people at the boat place how we need to get onto 77."

That's good news. A man wanting to ask for directions, which isn't a common thing in my experience. I enthusiastically agree. "Sure, that seems the most sensible. It's amazing that once you get off the main roads here, how many smaller ones there are. and a lot without signs."

So we unanimously turn back round again and ride into a small car park in front of the boat dealership. This area in Alabama, I've noticed while crossing bridges, has a lot of remote waterways, lakes, and rivers. Walking into the dealership, a big red truck is parked up at the main entrance. I squeeze past, briefly looking into the truck and see in the front, resting on the front seat, two large rifles! This must be a place for hunting, too.

The showroom, feeling like it's in the middle of nowhere, is a little bizarre and like nothing I've seen before. Instead of expecting to see beautiful leisure boats like the one we'd been on back in Florida, while these are also flat bottomed, they look more like they've been built for a military mission. Some are painted in khaki stripes, others are all green, or all grey, or all brown to, I guess, simply blend into the countryside and waterside landscapes. In fact, these are boats made for the area, also flat hulled, to navigate shallow waterways, but used for the major pastimes of both fishing and hunting.

A big guy with an even bigger stomach and also dressed from top to toe in khaki, approaches us, but noticing we're carrying helmets probably doesn't think he'll be getting a quick sale from us for a boat. He kindly puts us back in the right direction, after looking at Mike's weather-beaten map.

Successfully on Route 77, another small road in the middle of nowhere, we're led through the beautiful Cheaha State Park, with its rolling ridges and tall pine forests and, amazingly, see a sign indicating, a few miles up, another road leading to Alabama's highest point of 2,407 feet. We continue passing through little farming towns aptly named, like Chandler Springs, Ashland, Mellow Valley, Milltown, and Almond.

Historically, a massive amount has happened in this area, too. We approach and stop at the famous Horseshoe Bend National Military Park. This is the site of the last battle of the Creek War on 27 March 1814. The Tennessee militia, aided by Cherokee and Lower Creek allies, finally crushed the Upper Creek Red Stick during the Battle of Horseshoe Bend, located here on the Tallapoosa River we're crossing. This battle broke the power of the Creek Nation and over eight hundred Upper Creeks died defending their homeland. Incredibly, this was the largest loss of life for Native Americans in a single battle in the history of the United States. Just five months later, in August, the Creeks signed a treaty and ceded an unbelievable twenty-three million acres (93,000 km2) of land in Alabama and Georgia to the United States government.

Towards the end of the morning, with the temperatures continuing to soar, we stop the bikes at a gas station in Lanett, just before entering Georgia, to get ourselves and the bikes filled up with gas and water, but not in that order. I'm not really sure what difference we'll see between the two states, but I do know that Alabama is a place that has deeply touched me, from seeing the impoverished small towns we've been through, but also meeting people providing the warmest hospitality and kindness.

Soon, not more than a few hundred yards from leaving quiet Lanett, we ride through West Point, on Georgia's state line, which leads us immediately over the Chattahoochee River out onto Georgia Route 18. It's here, too, that we loose an hour by leaving the Central Time Zone and now being in the Eastern Time Zone. Unfortunately, this means we'll have one hour less of daylight to travel and get to Valdosta before it gets dark.

I'm strangely excited to be in Georgia. Besides Atlanta, which I'd visited once to attend a trade show, not seeing much more than the inside of a conference centre and hotel, I know nothing about this state, but I do know, that some of my favourite songs and musicians have something to do with Georgia. Growing up, I'd often hear Gladys Knight and the Pips singing Midnight Train to Georgia, and who can't be moved by Randy Crawford's Rainy Night in Georgia or Ray Charles singing Georgia on My Mind, when he refused to play to segregated audiences here.

Riding along the field lined roads, Mike signals and pulls over. So I do the same, now, getting used to his spontaneous stops.

Mike reaches for his bottle of water from his tank bag and, after a big gulp, says, "So, we're now in Georgia or the "Home of Peaches." We're gonna head eastwards for a while and should look out for a place to maybe get a bite to eat for lunch. Manchester could be a good place. It's just thirty odd miles from here, and you'll feel like you've walked back in time there. I think there should be a couple of places we could check out there to grab a bite."

After another slurp of the water and wiping the back of his arm across his mouth, he adds "So, like I asked you in Alabama. Is there anything you want to try and see or stop off for?"

Not really knowing what could literally be 'round the corner, I just honestly reply, "Well, nothing, really, but if you see anything you reckon is worth stopping for I'll be on for that."

"OK, that leaves the plan pretty open, but I'll see what we can do. You know, this time of the year it's harvest time here, so there may be some interesting farm stands on the roadsides. Let's see what we find."

Mike quickly drinks the rest of his water, shakes the last remaining drops out of the bottle, and puts it securely back into his tank bag. Concluding that small interlude, we head eastwards on Route 18 through lush green fields and fertile hills, with the sounds of tractors and agricultural machines out in the distance. We have the road all to ourselves. Slowly going round a bend, and, before reaching the outskirts of Pine Mountain, I spot on the other side of the road a small, open-sided structure with a wooden slanted roof. Seeing what's piled on and around it makes us both immediately want to stop and pull over beside it.

Hundreds of enormous pumpkins of all varieties—bright orange, yellow, and white, some the size of beanbag chairs— are nestled on top of and between bales of straw. On top of the tables are boxes of beautiful red and green glossy apples and other sorts of small pumpkins, squash, and corn on the cob. I walk over, fascinated to see a small sign on the top of the counter with a small black box with the key in it next to it. It simply says, "Welcome to Pumpkin Patch. Please take whatever you want. The honor box is here for you to leave your contribution. Thank you."

I suppose the farmer or the farmer's wife can't stay around all day, in such a quiet place that hardly has any traffic going by, hoping someone will drop by, so they just have to trust that whoever comes by will pay for the produce they take. Apparently, this is quite normal around these parts.

I walk around towards the back and spot a massive, shiny orange pumpkin. I try and lift it off the ground. Impossible. But I can imagine that it would make a hell of a lot of pumpkin soup, if you could only get it into a truck and out again.

Ironically, just as I'm again trying to lift the pumpkin, a bearded guy in a tractor trundles up, smiling and waving over to us. "Good morning. Just come down from one of the fields up there and to check out some fencing on the other side here. Saw you folk. Need any help with the pumpkin?"

I turn around and smile and point to the bike, shaking my head.

"Oh, yea." He nods understandingly. "I guess that would make one hell of a heavy passenger. See you guys!" And with that, he's off at two miles per hour down the road.

Leaving my overweight orange pillion behind, but getting some apples and sliding a note into the honesty box, we continue along Route 18, through the green leafed and wooded roadside. Almost arriving at Warm Springs we come to the Franklin D. Roosevelt State Park. This is Georgia's largest park, covering more than 9,000 acres, with extensive hiking trails and rental cabins to stay in and a good spot to maybe do some fishing. Incredibly, within this park is Roosevelt's "Little White House", one of Georgia's most popular visitor attractions. Searching for relief from his polio, Franklin D. Roosevelt first came to Warm Springs in 1924 to swim in the springs' naturally heated water. Enchanted by the area, he built a very simple vacation cottage on the side of Pine Mountain, while running for President in 1932. Sadly, while posing for a portrait in his den, FDR suffered a stroke and died on 12 April 1945, towards the end of World War Two. The unfinished portrait is still on display there for people to see.

Continuing along, I literally start feeling my stomach begin to rumble, after only having had a chocolate muffin a lot earlier that morning. With just a few miles to go until we reach Manchester, I'm just hoping Mike was right when he said there should be a few places to eat there. But, from what I've seen, places, particularly in these kinds of areas, must surely "come and go." We arrive at what I guess is the town's central Main Street, but the place feels asleep. It's totally quiet, and the sound of our two bikes going down the street seems to be the only thing happening here. We ride down one side and see nothing that looks remotely like a place to eat, so we turn around and head back up on the other side. Nothing much.

A bit further up we pass a non-descript place, with white awnings hanging over and shading the windows and a piece of paper stuck on the window that maybe looks like a food menu. Curiosity gets the better of us. We park up. I quickly take my helmet off and, with my hair joyfully just a bit nice and sweaty now, hide it under a baseball cap. We walk over and peer through the window. This unassuming little place has nothing to distinguish it from the outside, except the little notice saying, "Tant's Cafe Serves All-U-Can-Eat today." Plainness doesn't mean it's ordinary, and I'm more than happy to go in, also maybe because it's the only place open.

We walk inside, and I'm immediately stricken by the austerity and simplicity of the place. Bare, long tables have just a few people eating from large trays, and it looks like there is no table service. We walk up to the "food bar" and see in front of us displayed large metal pots of vegetables, mashed potatoes, corn, macaroni, salad, bread, and gravy. There's also some fried chicken, some beef hash, and just a bit of meat loaf still left. The only menu is a large blackboard on the wall behind the counter.

Two smiling, old and rotund ladies, one White and one Black, are standing behind the counter, serving food into plates. One of them chirps up, "Well, hello, y'all. You take your time now and have a look at what we got. All cooked fresh today."

So we take a look, but, unsurprisingly, the choice is a simple one. It looks like people come here to eat a lot. The first choice is a "One Trip Special" at $7.35, which includes one meat, two vegetables, one bread, but drink is extra. The second choice is "All-U-Can-Eat" at $9.99, which includes the salad bar, the food bar, dessert, and drink. Not bad! Unfortunately, it's not Friday, otherwise we could have opted for a catfish "One Trip" or "All-U-Can-Eat" option. Interestingly, underneath the menu board, it mentions that Georgia State Law requires a clean plate on return trips to the food bar, and, no doubt from previous experience, they've added "No doggie bags are allowed on 'All-U-Can-Eat' plate options!"

The two ladies wait patiently, smiling for our big decision of one of the two choices. I go for the simple option, while Mike says he wants his plate to groan. I can see that there's got to be a story here, as I notice a painting of an old, but kind-looking gentleman hanging in a prominent position on the back wall behind them.

While I'm choosing my vegetables and the ladies are putting them into a compartmentalized plastic tray, I ask curiously more about Tant's.

One of them looks up, surprised I'm showing interest, wipes her hand down her apron, and puts it out to shake mine. "Well, I'm Miss Annie and this is Miss Joan. We both own this place equally now and have worked here for many years. When the owner, who we had worked a long time for, passed away, he left the place to us to look after. That's his picture up there. We're so indebted to him. So we try and help the community, and we would never refuse anyone without money or who couldn't afford to eat. We will give food to the poor to help out here."

This has just got to be the epitome of a soul food joint. I'm blown away by their kindness and humbly take my tray back to our table, where Mike has already started digging in. I tell him the story, and, with his mouth full and unable to speak, he just raises his eyebrows, which I think means he's duly impressed.

Before leaving, we take our trays back to Miss Annie and Miss Joan, who come round to give me a big hug and wish us a safe trip home. Wonderful people. With my stomach now a lot fuller and with no more rumbling, we walk out onto the hot Main Street, get on our bikes, and turn back round but almost come to a stop again. It's to admire an incredibly beautiful original white Art Deco building, or the "President Cinema." Why a building like this, of such class and style, in a place so austere and simple? I don't know, and Mike shrugs his shoulders, which I guess means he doesn't, either.

But Mike's looking impatient, like we've still got a long way to go. He looks up from his map. "We're gonna head south now on Georgia Route 41, then Georgia Route 26 to US 19 to Albany. Then it will be GA Route 133 all the way to our destination tonight in Valdosta. I do hope we get there before it gets too dark. It's still about another two hundred miles, and they're predicting it might start raining later down there. I've stayed with Julie, my old high school friend, before, but I can't quite remember where her exact street is. That's why it would be better if we can do it in daylight."

That last comment about the rain I don't want to even think about, having brought no waterproof gear with me from the

UK. Because of that deficiency, Mike had kindly provided me with what I can only describe as a massive XXL blue hooded plastic rain jacket. Not exactly what I'd call stylish or very flattering. Up until now, it hasn't seen daylight from my side saddlebag, and that's where I'm hoping it's going to stay.

The roads leading south towards the Georgia and Florida border are beautiful. The bikes are running wonderfully, and the warm breeze is brushing past my bare arms. Back to reality. Mike is still wearing his heavy-duty padded waterproof jacket. He must be hot. That's a stoic man for you!

Just south of Albany, we pass a little place called "Pecan City", which reminds me to keep an eye out for any road stands selling those lovely nuts, which cost a fortune back home. The skies are now ominously clouding over the nearer we get to Valdosta, with the sun slowly setting and creating a pink and red tinge to the darkening sky. I'm feeling like we need to get to our destination sooner, rather than later.

We finally see the welcoming signs of Valdosta, and then, in the almost darkness, it's just a question of riding back and forth through a number of long pine-covered roads with their lovely country southern homes for Mike to remember which one we'll be staying at!

We arrive just in time, as the clouds have totally blackened, and a few spots of rain are felt. The sound of the bikes in this quiet residential road awaken a couple of dogs, who come barking out to frighten or greet us. Mike seems to know them, and, even with his helmet on, they also seem to recognise him! One's a big heavy American Bulldog and the other what looks like a mix of German Shepherd and Corgi, who seem most excited running circles around us.

Julie also comes out to greet us and quickly ushers us towards her double garage, saying with slight concern, "Heavy rain is predicted tonight and tomorrow, so it's probably best you get your bikes in here to keep them protected. Those stormy winds can do damage, too, and might knock them over if they stay outside."

Mike smiles and nods in agreement, already quickly pushing his bike in and untying his bags. "Good idea. Thanks. You never can tell what kind of storms might come in."

I follow suit and heave my bag off, dropping it onto the ground but leaving the sexy rain jacket inside the saddle bag. With that, we follow Julie inside to her lovely house, and I'm immediately in my element admiring beautiful oil and acrylic canvases displayed on almost every square inch of her walls. Mike had mentioned she's a well-known artist and teaches at the local university and manages their gallery.

She looks over and smiles. "I can see you're interested by the art. Before anything else, you guys sort yourselves out. Zoë, your room is out the back overlooking the backyard and woods, next to my father, Jack. Just keep the door closed so the dogs don't go in, and, Mike, you have the choice of sofas here tonight."

I smile. Her style is bold, colourful, and dramatic of remote landscapes across America. Maybe a little reminiscent of the Post Impressionist, Paul Gauguin. "Sounds good. The colours and textures in your paintings are incredible. That massive one over there. Where and what is that about?"

"Oh, those are the swamplands down in Florida—an eerie place. Those trees just seem to survive in the water like stoic soldiers. If you like, we can wander out back into my art studio later, if you want to see some more."

I nod eagerly, but that's not before we're introduced to her dad and led into the kitchen, and a massive fridge, almost full of just beers, is opened, and bottles generously brought out to toast our arrival.

We all sit around the bar, and Jack asks inquisitively, "So, Zoë, how much do you know about this area of southern Georgia?"

"Honestly? Not that much, but I'd love to know a bit more. Time is never on our side to go visit everything in a place. It's always impossible. But I'd love to hear anything quirky about where we are. It's not a good night to be going out, with the coming storm, so some good stories would be great."

Mike nods in approval, like that's a good idea and sits back with a beer in his hand to listen to something that maybe even he's not heard before.

Jack, who I later learn is a bit of a historian and avid reader, smiles, rubbing his chin. "Well, you probably think that we live in the back of beyond, but Valdosta has a few celebrities and bits of history. Have you heard about the OK Corral?"

I nod enthusiastically. "I certainly have. Cowboys. Gunfights. But this doesn't seem like a very 'Western' kind of place."

He continues, "Well, there was a guy called Doc Holliday, an outlaw, a long time ago like Jesse James, who was a professional gambler and gunfighter. He's famous for the gunfight at the OK Corral and was a US Marshal in the American Old West. He lived in Valdosta when he was young. Our more recent cowboys here in Georgia were the Dukes of Hazzard, and that young deputy, Enos, who chased Bo and Luke, he lives here in Valdosta!"

He obviously wants to see I'm impressed, and, although I don't recognise all the names, I raise my eyebrows and nod slowly, with an impressed look. Spurred on, he continues, "And you must have heard the *Star Spangled Banner* being played? Well, Francis Scott Key wrote the poem, which later became the words for America's national anthem. It talks all about the bombardment of Fort McHenry by British ships of the Royal Navy in the Chesapeake Bay during the war of 1812. He's another one that lived for a while in Valdosta."

By now, Mike is also raising his eyebrows, which signals more from Jack. "Oh, and, if my memory serves me correctly, talking about music, strangely Jingle Bells was written here!"

Even Julie raises her eyebrows now at that one. We all giggle, but Julie's expression suddenly turns serious, and she walks over to the window to close the blinds from the darkness outside.

She sits back down and opens another beer, while putting more chips into a bowl. "Now, if you want to hear a story and a half, I've got one hell of a cracker that'll make you shiver. Here, close by, have been mysterious sightings of something which isn't quite normal. You must have heard of Big Foot, well there's something similar here called the 'Skunk Ape,' who we think lives near the Little River and woods here, and it's recently created a lot of national interest with a lot of sightings. Our local paper, the *Valdosta Daily Times*, has received calls from readers, who believe they have seen what may be a Skunk Ape here, of all places, in South Georgia. One report came from Brookes County, the other from Berrien County."

Even Mike looks mystified, like he's never heard about it before. "So Julie, what is it supposed to be and why's it called that? Strange kind of name."

Julie continues like she's stating a well-recorded fact, "Well, a Skunk Ape is, apparently, a hairy humanoid creature that walks on two legs. They say that it's similar to the legendary Big Foot, but of slighter build. Skunk Apes grow about seven feet tall and weigh two to three hundred pounds, according to witnesses. And the creature has that name because of the foul odour accompanying most sightings."

This is ridiculous. But we all nervously giggle.

"The smell is described as being similar to rotten eggs. Skunk Apes reportedly love wooded, swampy areas, like here, and the legend says they originally came primarily from the Florida Everglades. Believe it or not, there've been recent sightings from a couple of other sources I read about along the Withlacoochee River, between here in Valdosta and Quitman in Brookes County. Let me try and find that article, and I'll read it to you."

With that, she walks out with the dogs following, wagging their tails. A few moments later she returns with the local *Valdosta Daily Times* newspaper in her hand. She turns over some pages then props it up on the counter and puts her glasses on.

"Here we go. Listen to this and see what you think. It's hilarious, but we take it seriously. 'Between 10-10:30 PM Wednesday 21 April, Joy was driving along Highway 37, in Berien County. She had a friend on her cell phone. She had her car's bright lights on and she saw something hairy walking into the woods. She's quoted as saying, "I saw the back of something...it was tall...I thought it was a bear, but a bear doesn't walk on its back legs... honestly, it looked like an ape." Joy said her husband's about six foot tall, and she gauged that she saw it to be the same height. She didn't smell anything while driving by the creature. She then told her friend on the phone that she thought she'd seen something like a hairy man walking into the woods. Her friend laughed and asked if Joy had been drinking. Joy told the *Times*: "I told her I hadn't been drinking and anyway, Sir, I don't drink!"

"'A few days later a man in Brookes County claimed he also "saw it." Earlier in the year, before the leaves returned to the trees, he was smoking a cigar on the back porch of his home. Between 10-11 in the morning, he saw something walk out of the woods! He first thought it was a deer but saw it had no hind quarters. He then thought it's an idiot in a ghillie suit, which is a type of camouflage clothing, covered in loose strips of cloth or twine designed to look like foliage. But even then he thought something wasn't quite right. He went inside to get a pair of binoculars. He saw a hairy humanoid, with the hair being red, fading to brown and grey. He had a good sighting of it. He's quoted as saying that "the creature was probably about 500 yards away, too far to smell!"'"

Julie reads the next bit then chuckles. Listen to this. This is really funny: "He watched the creature for about eight minutes through the binoculars and said, "During that time, the creature leaned on one arm against a tree, looking around. It scratched its left calf with its left foot. Then it ran away. It didn't walk like a human." He believes the creature stays lean from eating meat. But what kind of meat? He's taking no chances and says, "If I go out in the woods now, I make sure to carry something with me that goes bang!" The paper ends the article by saying that there's probably at least another nine people who've seen it, but who haven't said a word to anyone because they don't want people thinking they're crazy!

We all sit back gob smacked and grab a few more beers.

Much later that evening, exhausted but exhilarated from what we've achieved that day, including the stories, we notice the dogs stand up and bark. We start to hear the ominous and vicious rumblings of thunder, with the rain starting to lash down onto the windows, and strong winds blowing through the trees in the backyard. We're not worrying. We're happy. We're safe and so are the bikes, even from the Skunk Ape!

9

GATOR HAT

Valdosta, Georgia, to Lake Wales, Florida

240 miles

Someone's loudly knocking on my bedroom door, and it's the middle of the night! I wake up startled, but what sounds like hammering is actually coming from outside. This is loud thunder like I've never heard before, and it's got to be directly overhead.

I put my head under the pillow, pull the duvet completely over me, and with a big sigh try to fall asleep again. Trying to desperately, and consciously, fall asleep must be one of life's most difficult challenges. And why does it always seem to happen when you need your sleep the most. Another noise finally wakes me up again just a few hours later. This time it's inside, and it's the dogs barking and pawing at my door. Surely it can't be time to get up. It's still dark.

I roll over and grab my watch. It is indeed time to get up and just past 6:30, the time Mike said we needed to get ready to leave on time. I walk sleepy-eyed into the bathroom, where the dogs, wagging their tails, desperately try and run in with me. I slam the door shut just in time and hear the paws scratching at the door. I look into the mirror. Not a pretty sight. It looks like I didn't get much sleep, staring at my ruffled hair and reddish eyes. I'm a bit annoyed, knowing that out on the road I'll need all the concentration and energy possible.

But walking into the shower, I smile. Next to it, a large panel of sculptured enamel covers the wall. It's a sensual, naked body of a very muscular man with biceps and buttocks to die for. Teasingly painted around it are the words: "Easy boy. Lust brings out all the presumptions in me." Whoever said a bathroom was predictable and boring.

Freshened up as much as possible with my hair combed down, I pull on my jeans and the rest of my gear and wander into the kitchen. Mike and Julie are sitting on the stools, drinking a fresh brew of coffee.

Julie looks over and smiles. "Morning, Zoë. Help yourself. I'll put some toast on. So how did you sleep, or is that a stupid question? The storm last night was pretty close, and the rain outside is still pelting down. Even the dogs don't want to go out."

I nod in agreement. "Yea, I have to say the storm was pretty frightening and so loud."

Julie kindly puts some toast, butter, and jam on the counter then seriously and questioningly looks at Mike. "The weather out there is bad. Why don't you just postpone the trip for a couple of hours, or at least until the worst of it has passed over a bit?"

Mike, as ever the stoic adventurer, takes a gulp of coffee and shakes his head like it's nothing out of the ordinary.

"No. It's gonna be fine. We've got good rain gear, and the route is pretty easy on the main roads today."

I look at him a little surprised and, half smiling, say, "You're always prepared for this kind of weather and all eventualities. I haven't seen that big padded jacket of yours come off once in all the days we've travelled together. But for me, unfortunately, it's a different story. All I've got on me are my thin waterproof trousers and that mammoth blue jacket you insisted I bring. I'm going to have to roll up its sleeves and then, no doubt, the rain will drip through and down into my gloves!"

Mike perseveres like he hasn't heard what I've just said. "Let's get breakfast done, pack the bikes, and then get ourselves prepped. At least the rain here is warm!"

With that, he pours himself another coffee. At the same time Julie's father walks in and sits down next to him. Mike pours him a coffee and looks curiously at what he's got under his arm. It has to be said that both Julie and her father, Jack, now long retired, are both incredibly talented bohemian artists. With a serious love of art and literature, there's joyfully plenty of it in large quantities everywhere here.

Jack smiles and, stretching over the counter, hands me a massive book. "Zoë, I know you were looking at the book shelves last night. I thought you'd like this one to take with you on your travels."

I smile. Perfect. I'm flattered, having not expected anything so thoughtful and generous. It's a limited and rare edition of the Complete Short Stories of Ernest Hemingway, a lot of which were previously unpublished. He was the true man of bravery and adventure. This will definitely make good travel reading.

I look at Mike, realizing that luggage space is at a premium. Mike reads my thoughts. "It's massive but I can wrap it in some clothes and wedge it in my pannier compartment."

I smile gratefully. "Thanks. Hopefully it won't get too damaged or wet."

Thankfully, we do wait a while longer, but there seems little respite from the rain pouring down outside. Mike thinks differently and walks impatiently to the sink, quickly washing his mug up like he's on yet another important mission. "OK. I think we can load the bikes and wheel them out."

Both Julie and I look at each other incredulously but follow him into the garage, where the door is buzzed up. It's still pouring heavily outside. I'm just afraid that all my luggage is also going to get soaked. But help is at hand. Julie walks to the back of the garage and rifles through masses of boxes and books.

She pulls out a pile of enormous big black plastic bags. "Hey. Look what I've got. It's what Dad and I use for wrapping up our canvasses when we have to transport and protect them. Let's do the same with your bags. So the North Face and my pull up banner bags are meticulously wrapped in plastic bin bags and sealed with sticky tape. The DIY job looks like it's going to do just fine. Maybe she should do the same with me to keep me dry! Everything is then loaded back on the bike, looking like it's also now carrying a massive plastic condom on the top.

I'm not going to say, for one moment, that I look anything like a Michelin man, but that's what I feel like, with the additional layers I've put on to keep warm and the massive, oversized plastic, blue dress-length jacket hanging off me. It's not a flattering look.

We give Julie and Jack a big hug thanking them for their generous hospitality and push the bikes out into the rain. Now is not the time to talk anymore.

The bikes are quickly started up, full light beams switched on, helmet faces pulled down, and we carefully leave the tree-lined street, avoiding large puddles and potholes in the road. Almost immediately, I'm already wiping my visor from the downpour, with steam building up from inside. Then soon, without much warning, we've jumped back onto a major highway, otherwise known as Interstate 75, which, if we were to follow it to the end, would take us all the way to Ft. Myers and Golden Gate then east into the Miami area and Everglades National Park.

Immediately, my long lost friends, the "Demon Trucks" appear and are spewing out rivers of rain on either side of their massive wheels. Even Mike slows down and is wisely taking it easy. I'm seeing his rear red light go on and off with him testing his brakes from time to time, which I also do. We sadly continue like this for fifteen to twenty miles, finally reaching the state line into Florida, where miraculously, the intensity of the rain suddenly diminishes until it's become just a slight drizzle, but the skies are still covered in dark clouds.

Outside Jasper, just over the state line, along the highway I see the perfect place we can stop to shake the rain off. It's one of those local roadside places that for the "out of towner" is there to create curiosity and fascination. And I've found my heavenly place which sells pecans, "The Pecan Outlet." Timing couldn't be better, as the harvesting is around this time in October.

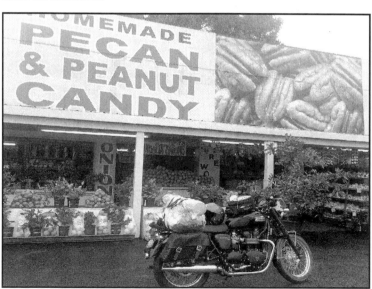

We park up outside. The rain has thankfully stopped, leaving just sodden, puddled roads, but which I'm sure will soon dry up when the clouds disappear and the sun decides to come out. I joyfully take off the Michelin jacket, shake it like "there's no tomorrow," roll it up, and put into the pannier. Hopefully that'll be the last time I do that. Au revoir mon ami!

I turn round and am greeted by an enormous sign above the yellow wooden, open-fronted shop. It simply says "Homemade Pecan and Peanut Candy. Tropical Honey & Jellies. Peach Cider"

Large bags stacked outside, filled with oranges and lemons, are nestled between potted orange and lemon trees. Even more oranges are piled high in pyramids on the counter space outside. We walk in, and on the tables in front of us are what I've been looking for—pecans, and of all sorts and descriptions: pecans with shells, pecans without shells, pecans encrusted with praline, and pecans covered in chocolate. No question. I'm going to get some for me and my family as Christmas stocking fillers. But I have to say, I'm surprised how expensive they seem to be. I was imagining getting bags for hardly anything, but here I pay out $8.99 for just a ten ounce pack of praline pecans.

We wander round this little place of treats, seeing shelves of jams, honeys, seashells, more pecans, and then things I've never seen before or even imagined would see on sale. I walk up closer to inspect. At the back of the shop are shelves covering from ceiling to floor, packed with alligator heads of every conceivable size, from one not much longer than my little finger to skulls that have got to be at least two feet long. They all have their jaws wide open with full sets of long, sharp teeth. I look along the shelves. Without hesitation, I pick up the largest one I can find. This is an opportunity too hilarious to miss. I look over to the girl at the counter with a questioning look, and she nods.

I walk outside and balance the alligator skull on top of my head, which goes down to almost cover my eyes. Mike is in his own world, self-absorbed, kneeling by his side bag and pulling out a cloth. I cough, and he turns around. Not only does he turn around, but he almost falls over in shock. "Oh my God, what are you doing? You look like a crazy monster. That gator's head is wild. Is it stuck?"

I can't help but laugh. "Thought that would surprise you. But I'm amazed how heavy it is!"

With that, he picks himself up and spontaneously takes his camera out. "Go sit on your bike with the gator head on. Looks like it's going to take the bike out for a ride!"

Besides the two small bags of pecans, I haven't been tempted to take the gator head, so that's left behind when we hit the road. With that, the sun suddenly appears from behind one of the clouds, and, all of a sudden, I feel like I'm truly back in sunny Florida.

So, give or take another two hundred miles, we jump back onto Interstate Highway 75 which runs right down through the middle of Florida. It's something we tried to avoid, but unfortunately, there really aren't any practical alternative smaller, parallel roads. We cruise at a steady sixty-five to seventy miles per hour along the flat, straight highway, passing Lake City and Gainsville. Halfway along we stop for fuel at Ocala.

At Love's Gas Station, while filling up, a large luxury truck pulls in, which looks like it's got some quality horses in it. Walking inside the store I see shelves of magazines related around this area's favourite subject—horse racing and breeding.

Apparently, Ocala has one of the largest number of thoroughbred breeding farms anywhere and is well known as a "horse capital of the world," with an incredible 1,200 horse farms. Ocala is also one of only five cities in the world (four in the US and one in France) permitted to use this prestigious title based on revenue produced by the horse industry.

Apparently, in this area alone 44,000 jobs are sustained by breeding, training, and the equine industry. Sounds like a good place to me. And there's further proof as we leave, going past and seeing fields full of horses grazing in them.

I have to say, the trip back is fairly non-descript, as we quite simply just have to get the miles under our belts, but, luckily, without any major mishaps and, besides the blistering heat and stopping from time to time for water, we hit the outskirts of Orlando by early afternoon.

Having left Route 75 and jumped onto Highway 27 via the Florida Turnpike just before hitting Orlando, we continue leisurely along it until we reach the outskirts of Lake Wales. From here, instead of taking the direct route back, Mike makes a small diversion, and we find ourselves riding parallel along some railway tracks. It's then that I see Mike signalling to turn into a motorbike repair shop and garage. Maybe he needs some parts. But it's not for that he's stopped. A bizarre piece of Americana is displayed blatantly in front of us.

Mike gets off his bike, takes off his helmet and points at it smiling. "I thought you'd like to see this although it was a bit out of our way. I don't reckon you'd see anything like that back in London and there's certainly nothing like it on Route 66!"

And I think he's right. Proudly displayed in the centre of the forecourt, on a large pedestal, is a massive, probably twenty foot long, black metal handgun, pointing out to the road. Why it's there, we can't fathom, but, apparently, it's been there for a long time. Unfortunately, the store is closed, so I'm not even able to wander in and curiously ask all about it. A mission no doubt for Mike when he's got a spare moment in the future. And then, quite literally, a great photo shoot opportunity has to be aborted. As I recklessly try to scramble up onto the gun barrel, it's just too high and slippery, and I fall onto my backside. This time it's Mike having the last laugh.

Mike jumps back onto his bike. "OK, enough tomfoolery, we need to get back and you need to sort your stuff out for tomorrow and try to find a place to stay down in the barrier island area offshore from Sarasota.'

"Yes. I'm going to get onto it when we get back. It sounds just like the sort of place I want to get to and chill out for a few days. I'll do some research and book something when we get back."

"And I'll draw you a detailed map on how to get there. It's really easy."

We bike past the vast water expanse of Lake Wailes and the playing pitches but not before coming to an emergency stop just before the house. Out in front of us in the road are two spectacular grey, long necked and red headed birds known as Sandhill Cranes. They are literally performing a beautiful "dance" intertwining their necks and jumping up and down flapping their wings. They casually look our way and, with a loud, harsh cackle, walk casually and very slowly off the road up onto the sidewalk, like they're in total control of the traffic around here.

Finally parking the bikes up on the grass, outside the garage, I once again unstrap and take off the plastic embalmed luggage. It looks in pretty good shape, with no massive rain damage, and the sun and wind while going down the highway have already totally dried it up.

Once inside, I search online and manage to find a few places which appear right on spec for where I want to stay and then get incredibly lucky with a last minute cancellation of a room that goes directly out onto the beach! So that's all sorted.

Shortly after, the kids are back from school and giggle when their dad tells them the stories about the gator hat and me falling off a gun. But I think they're actually sad and disappointed that we didn't in reality bring a gator head back with us.

Later that evening, while we're drinking beers on the porch, Jacob runs up and pulls me by the arm saying enthusiastically, "Hey, I really want to go and watch the football game tonight. It's just starting and my school's playing. You should come and watch it. Do you know how to play it?"

His parents smile, and I add, for what it's worth, "Well actually we don't play that game in the UK, although I think we have something similar called Rounders. I used to play that at school. But I'd be really interested to watch it and hear from you how it's done here."

So we all walk over to the football field across the road and climb the steep steps of the stand into the spectator seats. Lots of families and children have done the same, and it feels like one big community. As the sun slowly goes down and the big surrounding stadium lights come on, the teams appear, and the crowd cheers loudly. Mike passes round a massive tub of popcorn, and we all begin to enthusiastically clap as the game starts, and I just hope I'll understand what's happening.

10

BARRIER ISLAND PARADISE

Lake Wales, Florida, to Longboat Key, Florida

110 miles

I walk barefooted out onto the grassy front of the house
and breathe in deeply the warm, early morning air. The
seagulls are swooping and flying in large circles high overhead
in the deep, blue cloudless skies. It's going to be a good day to
travel over to the coast.

I climb back up the steps and sit down in the rocking chair
on the porch. I pull out from my pocket the bit of paper that
had been ripped out of a school exercise book. On it is a map
that Mike had roughly hand drawn last night. It's cute. It
has all the details I need, including neatly drawn pictures of
showing me where to go; the playing fields, a purple house,

the lake shore, railroad track, a lake, and a McDonalds, where I'll need to turn to go south.

I'm really not that good with my sense of direction, so visual aids with a simple cartoon map like this will definitely help in finding landmarks along the way. It's also only going to be about a hundred miles to get to where I'm going, so, within a few hours, I should be seeing the sea and making the most of exploring the area. I smile. I actually said, "Only one hundred miles!" That's nothing here in the US.

I fold the piece of paper carefully back into my trouser pocket and see Mike walking out, holding two mugs of coffee. He hands me one. "Hi, Zoë. It's a good morning to get out over to Sarasota. The temperature is still going to be in the low 80s and there's no forecast of rain." He continues, smiling, "but you can still take that blue waterproof dress if you want."

"Thanks, but I think I'll be just fine. I've just been looking at the map you gave me, and I'm fairly confident I'm going to be able to find my way."

"I promise you. It couldn't be easier. You head out of here and jump south back onto US 27, then at Avon Park it's west, west, west, and still west, on the same road until you can't go any farther and you hit water! Do you want me to wheel the bike out for you?"

I smile and gratefully nod. "Yes that would be kind. I'm taking a lot less gear with me this time as it's only for a couple of days, so the bag will be a lot lighter to carry around. Just a few clothes and a swimming suit. I can't wait to take a dip in the sea and just chill by the beach."

It was true. The luxurious notion of spending a couple of days of freedom by the sea and having no time schedule, commitments, or massive long distances to cover seemed grand to me. I had, after all, taken the last remaining two weeks of my annual vacation from the company for this trip, so some of the time should at least be spent relaxing and charging my batteries. I also knew, upon returning to Lake

Wales, that we'd then have a frantic few days biking back and forth to Orlando for the bike show there.

With the bag tied down with the Rokstraps and ready to leave, I start the bike but not before Mike points with his right index finger and says, "Don't forget to turn right at the purple house to get you onto the highway and then head south. We'll see you in three days for the show. Have fun!"

With that, he waves me goodbye, and I'm back out on the road on my own. I hope I'll be OK with the bike. But what joy! What undiluted and total freedom! The bike is also purring contentedly, feeling, I'm sure, that we're going to have a good ride out together. I've put the little piece of paper in my tank bag and look down at it. Right, let's concentrate as it's now me responsible for finding the way. No more Road Dog leading the way.

So, we've turned right out of the house, passed the playing fields, and now I need to turn right past the lake shore park. Ah, and here's the big purple house on the corner that Mike was talking about where I have to make another right. Now this looks familiar. I ride up Central Avenue, over the railroad tracks, remembering to stand off my seat like I'd seen Mike do, and to the end of the road, where I notice the McDonalds that had also been drawn on the map. I immediately turn left and jump onto US 27 South.

Phew! I'm already proud of myself that I've got this far without even having to ask anyone if I'm going in the right direction.

With the smoothness of the quiet highway, I quickly kick the gears upwards until I'm doing a comfortable sixty-five miles per hour. That's plenty on a morning like this with no rush.

I just feel the sensation of the warm wind blowing past and around me, see the green fields on either side, and know at this very moment in time I'm a totally free spirit, responsible to no one but myself. I'm almost feeling that with the speed and the wind brushing all over me that it's cleansing my fears, palpitations, and worries away. I know only too well that back home and facing "reality," I currently have a lot to deal with, and, potentially, my life path is needing to be dramatically changed. This was also one of the reasons that had convinced me to come over—to escape from the day to day pressures of a nine-to-five office job that were increasingly starting to worry and stress me out. I needed to stand back from things and look at them from a distance.

Hopefully, these next few days of quietness and solitude will help me clarify what I need to do to make a better, more fulfilling life for myself.

The miles on the speedometer quickly click away, and, within just half an hour or twenty-four miles to be exact, I exit at Avon Park, turning right, which will lead me westwards onto a tiny country road. Interestingly, it's a nice little town with its nickname agreeing—"City of Charm." It's also aptly named after the town of Shakespeare, Stratford-upon-Avon, where a large majority of the settlers came from. But I don't notice any Shakespearean Globe Theatre here!

Within a few minutes of riding through the main, central street, it gently merges into little Florida Route 64, where I feel I'm being transported back in time. Small farmsteads appear from time to time along this quiet country back road, with tractors and farm equipment parked up in the front of farms and cows grazing contentedly in the lush, fertile fields and birds flying and nesting in the trees.

There seems to be an abundance of rich biodiversity here, and I see signs for the Highlands Hammock State Park, farther south on US 27. I'd heard Mike talking about this place and thought I'd try and see it on the way back. It's one of Florida's oldest parks that opened in 1931 with cypress swamplands, pine flatwoods, and 1,000 year old oak trees. Apparently, black bears and Florida panthers can occasionally be seen, as well as alligators, turtles, and deer. I don't see any of them.

But it is hot! I pull over at the little place of Zolfo Springs, unbuckle the straps from the saddlebag, and get out a bottle of water and thirstily gulp it down. I pour some of the water onto the clean cloth, also taken from my bag, and wipe it over my face, which feels good. I then liberally apply my suntan lotion to my arms and face, and I'm all set again.

Passing over US Route 17, the road becomes ever smaller and quieter, with no towns or communities—just massive stretches of fields and swampland. I finally notice that the thirty-six mile long Manatee River has joined us and is following alongside the road. It will ultimately finish its journey flowing out into the Gulf of Mexico. Again, this river has an incredible bio-diversity, attracting wildlife, including more alligators, herons, manatees, dolphins, and fish, such as bass and catfish. It's even been said that bull sharks have occasionally been found in the brackish waters near its low lying outlet at the southern edge of Tampa Bay, close to where I'm going in Bradenton.

Bradenton will very quickly be the next town I'll be reaching, but not before I fully absorb and appreciate this wonderful ride along wild Route 64.

I think I've said it before, but I'm always expecting the places to be a lot smaller than they turn out to be in America. That's probably because I don't see it on sat-nav, so have no idea of scale. Bradenton is no exception. Very quickly the quietness and tranquillity of the roads disappear, and I'm pulled almost immediately into a busy two-lane expressway with retail outlets of every description on either side of this grassy-edged and manicured highway.

It's still only mid-morning and even too early to check in at where I'm staying, so maybe a little stop here would be a good idea. I haven't actually got a large map of Bradenton, but, if I can find a few people to ask, there's a couple of things I'd like to see to get a feel of the place. Hopefully, there will also be a half-decent coffee shop. It should only be a short diversion before I head over the bridge to Anna Maria Island and on to Longboat Key and Sarasota.

It's then that I see signs for Bradenton Riverwalk and then, with a bit of luck, notice a convenient place to park the bike next to a large outdoor retail outlet. I lock up my helmet in its bag on the bike, put on my sunglasses, and take a leisurely stroll. It's good to stretch the legs. Lots of people seem to have the same idea and are strolling towards the newly built two year old Riverwalk, on the southern shore of the Manatee River. This is beautiful, and the river looks enormous on this scenic, mile long walkway and park. Skateboarders, laughing kids splashing in the fountain, and families enjoying a day out confirm Sarasota's sister city as the "Friendly City".

After a while, having drank the last of my water, I'm getting thirsty and head back to downtown and walk along to discover beautiful Old Main Street, where dappled, tree lined pavements are alive with restaurants, shops, and cafes. I sit down at a table outside one and under an umbrella drink the best cappuccino this side of the Manatee River.

I'm feeling relaxed here, with the pace of things slowing me down, but I'm also still itching to finally cross the bridge and get out to Longboat Key. What I'm expecting I'm not quite sure, but, hopefully, the sand will be white and the sea will be blue.

I walk back to the bike, unlock my helmet, and get back onto the palm lined road out of Bradenton, which, amazingly, is still on Route 64, which, as Mike said, will finally end at Holmes Beach overlooking the sea on Anna Maria Island.

Immediately leaving the built-up town, a huge bridge appears and takes me out and over the beautiful bay area where boats are out sailing, across two small parts of the mainland, and finally out over the Anna Maria Sound waterway to the keys hugging the mainland coastline.

Looking on the local map, "Sun Coast Attractions", which I'd been given on Old Main Street, I can clearly see it's now easy to get to where I'm going. In fact, there's no choice. There's only one road—Florida Route 789 southwards, along the entire length of the keys. Where I am currently, it's better known as Gulf Drive. Already, there's a different feel here from the mainland. It's a small seaside resort with a slow moving pace and people carrying sun chair loungers and bags down to the beach. But I have to say a little too commercial, even here, for my liking, with tacky seaside paraphernalia shops every side of the street, and my dream of no-one but me, besides the palm trees, is far from reality here. Maybe I am just expecting too much.

I continue down to Bradenton Beach and see much of the same: holiday condos, hotels, and more tacky seaside stores. Don't get me wrong; it's not bad. It's far from that, but not what I'm looking for.

Just a couple of miles farther, it's not until I cross over the water on Longboat Pass and onto Longboat Key and the Gulf of Mexico Drive that I start to somehow see glimmers of hope in what I've been dreaming to find. This is looking pretty good! Along this palm lined road, I can see and smell the "good life." On my left, looking onto Sarasota Bay, are beautiful residences with their own boat moorings. On the other side, on my right, is the Gulf of Mexico and the open expanse of sea, with small condos and holiday cottages going directly onto the beach. A lot more refined and less populated.

I'd better pull out the address of where I'm staying, as I know I can't be that far away. I'll need to keep an eye out for number 5451. The numbers are decreasing, which is a good sign, and I'm on the right side of the road—on the Gulf side. And there I see it, The Sandpiper Inn.

I signal right and pull into the sandy, covered parking area. It's not even midday. I pull my bag off, check my face in the mirror that it hasn't attracted too many bugs, and walk up the little pathway through tropical scented gardens to a little cottage door that says "Reception – Please ring bell". I do as it says,; a dog barks from inside, and the door opens.

A lady appears, having stepped over a little grilled gate inside, which obviously is there to keep the dog away. "Good morning. How can I help?"

"Morning. I booked two nights with you at short notice yesterday, and you'd said you had a beach front studio I could take."

She puts her glasses on and looks at the little black book on her desk. "Are you Zoe Carnow? That's fine. You need to walk down through the gardens to the beach, and your studio is just there on its own with the patio outside. It's pretty quiet here now. We only have eleven rooms, so we've done you a deal. Normally, it would be lot more in peak season."

I can't believe my luck and smile appreciatively. She goes on to say, "Here's your key. The bed has been done, and the kitchen area has a fridge and oven, if you want to cook. We have a corner store, and the Blue Dolphin, across the road, does great breakfasts. Just ask me later if you need to know anything else."

"Thanks. I'm probably going to buy some food. Where's the best place you can suggest?"

Her eyes light up. "Ah! We've just had a new supermarket open in Bay Isles Parkway, just about four miles down the road. Look out for signs Publix. They've got great food, and the CVS Pharmacy is just next door to it. And, of course, if you wanna eat out, there's plenty of good places around here."

"That's great. I might just ask you for some ideas later. Somewhere good for seafood would be just up my street!"

I take the key and walk through the pretty little gardens with a pond and fountain, little guest cottages on one side with loungers in their flowered sun decks, and directly in front of me on the walkway I see palm trees and pristine white sand. I walk to the edge of the pathway and look onto the beach, which seems to go on for miles on either side. I look again to double check and see that it's completely empty. There's not a single other person here. Next to me is a small, low wall patio with long reclining sun chairs. This is the place. Not bad! I walk into the air conditioned room, which is far bigger than I need, and flop down onto the king size bed. How good is this? I can't help but smile.

But still needing to get back on the bike to hunt for food, I leave the bag in the room and walk back outside to the bike. But first I walk to the edge of the empty beach and look out to the aquamarine sea. I bend down and run my fingers through the warm, finest of fine, white sand grains. It feels like pure decadent luxury in what I'm doing, and I'm already visualizing doing the same very soon with my bare feet.

The seat of the bike is now pretty hot, so, reluctantly but with no other choice, I jump quickly back on and ride the couple of miles along the beautiful, scenic Gulf of Mexico Drive, where luxurious residences and enchanting golf courses live side by side and next to the sea.

I pull up in front of Publix Supermarket, expecting nothing but the best in this sort of place. I'm looking forward to grabbing a trolley and browsing the aisles for some good food to take back. The idea of getting some fresh, tasty food for lunch and tonight sounds like a perfect plan. I can even indulge in a good bottle of wine, as I won't have to get back on the bike later tonight. This place is to die for, and I'm not disappointed. I always love going into American supermarkets, where the choice and presentation of fresh foods is second to none. The salads, fruit, and vegetables are being finely sprayed over with chilled water to keep them fresh and cool. I don't know why this isn't done in England. I'm having a field day, but, being only too aware that I can't carry that much back on the bike, I shop wisely, stocking up with local raspberries and strawberries, mango, pate, salad stuff, avocado, prawns, crab, fresh baguette, some yoghurt maybe for breakfast, more pecans, freshly squeezed carrot juice, and a fine bottle of Californian white—perfect.

I carry the two brown paper bags under my arms to the bike, which has been parked just outside, and methodically re-pack the side panniers with the delicious food and drink.

I'm back within ten minutes and walk through the tropical garden feeling and smelling the warm sea breeze. The food's placed in the fridge, and I open my bag, rummaging for my bathing suit and towel. I'm now going to indulge in self-made decadency. I quickly get changed, grab my sunglasses, a bottle of carrot juice and suntan cream, and, with the Ernest Hemingway book under one arm, walk barefooted out onto the sandy beach. I just stand there for one minute wriggling my toes up and down feeling the warm grains slide through them.

I look up at the sky, putting my glasses on, and see not a single cloud. I promise you, living in the UK really makes you appreciate simple things like that, when most of the time our skies are continually covered in them. I unwrap my towel from around my waist and lay it on a reclining sun chair. I dump everything else onto it and drag it down close to the lapping, warm water's edge.

Falling back onto the lounger with my feet dangling from the end of it, I look out to sea, watching the waves and foamy white horses come crashing onto the beach. I slowly close my eyes, feeling the warm sun on my skin and hear nothing but the repetitive sounds of the sea, with its waves coming onto the beach, moving the shells and fine shingle back and forth, in and out. The repetitive sounds are like a mantra dispelling any tension, and I lie motionlessly in complete peace.

After a while, I open my eyes, and, directly in front of me, a handful of birds are running back and forth across the beach near the water's edge. They are no more than six to eight inches long, with streaky brown upper parts, white bellies, and long legs. These are the famous sandpipers, a small wader and shorebird that seems to chase the waves away to then probe with their beaks the wet mud and sand for food. It's quite comical as I sit quietly watching them. Every time waves come pounding in, the sandpipers leave it to the very last moment to run away and escape from them. At that very moment, I get up and walk down to the water's edge, and the sandpipers run down the beach, out of my way. I put my feet into the warm water, and it laps up and around them. I walk further in through the waves and fall back, floating on the bobbing water. I take a few strokes and body surf back to the beach. That bit of energy has created a bit of hunger, so I grab the towel and walk back to the cottage. I rustle up a pate and salad baguette sandwich and wander back with it onto the beach.

They do say that sometimes some of the simplest things in life are the best. Walking through the sand, sitting back in the lounger, eating simple food, and watching the sea are just some of them.

Time runs away, and, before I've even opened the book to read Ernest's adventures, the sun starts to go down, and I know it's time to walk back up the beach.

That evening, the sunset is spectacular, with a red and orange sky and the stars quickly starting to peep out one by one. A lot later, I sit back outside on the terrace, with a glass of wine in one hand, and become mesmerized by the massive universe above me.

11

SARASOTA CIRCUS

Longboat Key, Florida, to Sarasota, Florida

Just a few miles

The sandpipers are running in and out of the water's edge
as I perch on the terrace wall, with my feet in the sand looking
out to the turquoise sea, holding a cup of coffee in one hand
and a local map in the other.

Overhead, several giant white pelicans are flying in
military precision, flapping their massive wings then suddenly
bombing down to catch the fish under the sea's surface. I look
curiously up and down the long stretch of beach, and, besides
a couple of people jogging, far out into the distance I have this
place all to myself.

I wander back in and put fresh fruit, nuts, and yoghurt
into a big bowl and sit back outside, mulling over how I'm

feeling and what I'd like to do. You see, that's me all over! I've got this permanent strap line buzzing away in my head that "life is too short, and you've got to make the most of it" but sometimes to the detriment of resting up.

I only have just one more day in this beautiful tropical place, which, at the moment, seems like another world and a million miles away from the damp, dark London I recently left. I really want to get onto that gorgeous, sexy bike and twist its throttle down the keys to Sarasota. Yes, that's it! A nice leisurely ride, mooze around to soak it all up, and then maybe find an interesting place to eat out later.

Dropping the key off this time, in addition to the barking dog, I'm greeted by a smiling guy in a dressing gown. "Morning, Ma'am. So, you've got your day planned out?"

I nod, "Just a short ride today down to Sarasota. Anything I should see?"

He rubs his chin and ties his robe belt in tighter, like he wasn't expecting anyone to knock on the door. "Well, depends on how much time you've got, but I'd try and stop at St. Armands Key, then maybe head over to Main Street in Sarasota to take a walk. Always stuff happening over there."

Smiling, I thank him. I walk out to the empty car park and, approaching the bike, do the habitual malarkey of casually kicking the tyres just to make sure. It just reassures me, don't ask me why, that somehow they haven't become flattened, punctured, or knifed overnight. Bizarre, I know! But true.

It's perfect weather, warm and balmy, with the bike's chrome and black paint shining brightly in the sun. Without the heavy luggage and tank bag on, it looks perfectly sleek and elegant—just like this place. I've also made an effort, and, with a nice clean white T-shirt and jeans and just a little bit of lipstick, I put my helmet on, pull the sun visor down, and kick it into first.

I look down at the odometer. It looks like I'll need to fill up. So, first job of the day will be to keep an eye out for a gas station. I look left, then right, then left again, wait for a convertible red Mustang to go past, then pull out of the driveway turning right.

The road is straight, with immaculately kept cut grass verges and swaying palm trees lining it. Between the buildings on my right, I catch glimpses of the blue sea, and, on the other side, the quieter waters of the Bay. I go past the supermarket I went to yesterday and continue past a golf course, where players in their buggies are already out chasing their balls.

It's there, just across the road, that I quickly catch sight of a Mobile gas station. Not wanting to miss the opportunity, I signal quickly, cross the road, and ride into the forecourt. It's a small place with just two pumps, but more than enough for me. I walk in to pay, picking up a local newspaper, thinking it might just give me ideas on where to go today and maybe go and eat tonight. I hand over a ten dollar bill and wait for the change from the guy behind the counter.

"There you go," he says, counting the dollar bills into my hand.

"Thanks. I'm staying locally here for a couple of nights, and tonight I was trying to find a really nice local place that serves good seafood. Anything you can recommend?"

He smiles knowingly and points his finger to his chest. "You've asked the right person. and you're in the right place! One of the best places here in Sarasota for food and location, and a bit of a hidden secret, is just down this small road to the dock. I don't know if you're going to be able to get a table tonight. Better you call them. They're the only place down there. The Dry Dock Waterfront Grill, next to the boat yard, and they bring in fresh fish every day. The views out across the bay are very pretty in the evening, looking out over to the Sarasota city skyline. Try and get a table outside, overlooking the boats."

That's a great piece of local advice and definitely not a place I'd have automatically ridden past. Seems like a plan. I jot the name down on the back of the gas receipt and, smiling, stuff that and the dollar bills into my jeans pocket.

Handing the pen back, I say, "Thanks. I'll give them a call later."

Turning left out of the forecourt and continuing past the elegant and challenging links-style Longboat Key Golf Club, and the tree-lined sister Harborside Golf Course on the other side of the road, I pass over another small bridge and onto a narrow strip of road with water on either side. I'm now on St. Armands, another wealthy looking key, and, continuing up the road, I arrive at its centre, St. Armands Circle, a luxurious tree encircled enclave with a beautiful park in the middle. In Britain we'd call this a massive roundabout, but I don't think that word is fully descriptive or stylish enough for here. All the way around, lining the circular road, are shops, art galleries, restaurants, and cafes. This looks good and feels very wealthy.

I ride slowly round once, absorbing the refined atmosphere but at the same time trying to look around to see where the hell I can park up. It's while doing this that I notice elegantly dressed, bejewelled, sun-glassed individuals curiously peering over their cappuccinos and newspapers wondering, "Who's the girl on the motorbike?" Well, that's what I think. The place is busy, and cars are parked tightly tail to tail. Whatever I do, I can't make a cock up with parking the bike and looking like a twat.

Already starting my second lap around the Circle, I quickly notice a small space between a silver Mercedes and black Corvette in front of Cafe l'Europe, where everyone is sitting outside watching the world, and me, go by. OK, so how am I going to get into this small space quickly and tidily while feeling everyone's looking at me? I stop horizontally in front of the Corvette, put the bike into neutral and, still sitting on it, slowly push its heavy weight back with my feet between the two sparkling, still unscratched cars. Not bad, if I say so myself and perfectly positioned facing outwards to get out easily.

I look up at the street notice and see if there are any parking restrictions or anything to pay. As long as I'm back in a few hours there'll be no problem. I lock my helmet onto the bike and, walking between the traffic coming anti-clockwise round the circular road, cross over to the island to take a better look. It's a beautiful park with immaculate flower borders and tropical plants. Looking down towards my feet I see a multitude of large bronze wheels firmly embedded in the ground and in a big circle. I look a little closer and see that on each of them are different intricate engravings of tigers, elephants, clowns, acrobats, trapeze artists, and multitudes of other circus characters. A little surreal. Below each wheel is another plaque explaining the troupe or person it represents. I realize I'm in the "Circus Ring of Fame."

St. Armands Circle was actually one of John Ringling's creations. Ringling was an Iowa-born circus owner, whose phenomenally successful show made him a multi-millionaire. He purchased the island in 1917 and produced an adventurous plan for a housing development, which centred on a circular shopping mall featuring gardens and classical statues. Like many places, this area flourished briefly before being caught up in The Great Depression. Fortunately, it was brought back to life in the 1950s and now looks very much as Ringling had planned, with its shady avenues radiating from this central point.

The Sarasota area has a rich circus heritage, with the famed Ringling Museum in the town. Each wheel, and there must be hundreds, recognises all those who have made a significant contribution to the art and culture of the circus from around the world.

Started in 1987, each year Ring of Fame candidates are nominated by the public, and then a corresponding individual wheel is presented. Reading the plaques conjures up memories of circus greats, such as famed animal trainer Gunther Gebel-Williams and the clowns Lou Jacobs and Emmett Kelley. The Ring includes the most famous showmen of all times. PT Barnum and the visionary who brought the circus to Sarasota, John Ringling.

I cross back over the road and stroll around the circle of shops from high class jewellers to, unfortunately, more touristy, cheaper stuff, which I'm seeing everywhere I go. There is, however, one of those places I just have to stop at to take a closer look and have a little giggle. On the window is a photograph of a mermaid with long blond hair lying on a beach. The words below say, in all seriousness: "Hand crafted swimmable mermaid tails made to order for adults or children. Perfect for that special occasion or just lounging on the beach! Tails can be worn in the water. We also rent professional mermaids!" Only here!

That reminds me. Some fresh fish for lunch would be nice. Just a little bit further up, I notice a welcoming restaurant, the Columbia, with huge open windows that connect a hand painted, tiled dining room to a sprawling outdoor covered patio with the wonderful smell of food wafting out. I curiously walk over to the menu on the wall—a mix of Spanish and Cuban fare. I look down the list; yum! Paella, packed with fresh clams, shrimp, and mussels; bean soup with chorizo; snapper; chicken and rice; and Cuban bread. Below, at the bottom, it claims to be the oldest restaurant in Sarasota, serving food since 1905. So, surrounded by the Circle's paradise of lush tropical landscaping and smartly attired waiters, I take a seat outside, now also having a prime view on what's going on, including seeing curious people going up to take a closer look at the bike.

The choice is any easy one, a selection of mouth watering tapas—fried octopus, prawns on the shell, and roasted peppers, then a local white fish with red onions, avocado, olives, tomatoes, and oranges on a bed of chive mashed potato. Delicious, with the true flavours and colours of this place. Unfortunately, I need to get back on the bike afterwards, otherwise I would definitely have had one of those small jugs of sangria I saw being served onto almost every other table.

Just watching the spectacle of these eclectic people walking past in this sophisticated place is the equivalent of a dessert of delicious voyeurism. Truly contented, I walk back to my two wheels to still happily see a few people passing by giving it their smiles of approval. I smile back, squeeze the bike out from the two beautiful cars, and head over to downtown Sarasota for a quick visit before planning to be back on the beach later in the afternoon.

I ride over Coon and Bird Keys and make my way to Sarasota's Main Street to take a stroll and walk off my lunch. Again, it's a place bustling with sophistication, and I can also see and understand now why it's Florida's cultural Mecca. There's a professional opera company, orchestra, ballet, and a multitude of theatres, music, and dance troupes in this town. Along Main Street, I see panels and posters advertising some of these events. Besides the cultural stamp, it's accumulated a number of other identities, from a fabulous beach getaway destination, with the Siesta Key Beach down the road ranked number one in the USA in 2011, to a thriving artists' colony, with its museums and galleries, and, of course, it's a circus town.

John Ringling, who created the circus culture here, was one of the many influential people attracted to the up and coming town in the early 1900s. Ringling poured money into the area, and his legacy is all around, nowhere more so than his house and fine art collection. In 1925, he decided to build an art collection and a museum to house it. He and his wife, Mable, had a strong affection for Italy, and their magnificent Italian Baroque paintings are the cornerstone of the collection. The famed Ringling Museum, the current home of his extensive art collection, is located on the grounds of his vast Venetian-Gothic thirty-two room mansion and winter residence, Ca' d'Zan, on Bay Shore Road. When Ringling died in 1936 it was bequeathed to the State of Florida.

This town also has a pretty quirky history, as I find out walking past a clothing store for golfers, where I read something I knew nothing about or wouldn't have even imagined. As we know, most towns grow from central squares or markets, busy ports, or intersecting highways, but Sarasota, unbelievably, they say grew up from a golf course.

In 1886, the town's founder, a Scot named J. Hamilton Gillespie, built the area's first course, a fairway with a green on each end. That fairway would eventually become Main Street, where I am today, in the heart of Sarasota. It would be the first of a further eighty-five courses, which would be created in the Sarasota and neighbouring Manatee counties.

From the small amount I've seen of the place, Sarasota seems to have a great combination of everything and seems pretty perfect to me.

But time is not on my side, and I'm feeling the urge again to walk through the sugar soft white quartz sand and float on the emerald green waters back on Longboat Key. I also need to book a table at the restaurant that was recommended to me this morning. I remember I'd written the number on the gas receipt and, walking down the street, call the number on my phone. It rings out. "Dry Dock Grill. Can we help you?"

I stop in the street and put a finger into my other ear to better hear the conversation above the noise of the traffic and shout, "Hi. Are reservations being taken for tonight?"

"Sorry, but we're afraid we don't take reservations for less than eight people. You just need to turn up. If you arrive just after seven, that should be fine. And are you arriving by boat or car? Do you want us to organise a mooring for you?"

That last question amuses me, feeling that they must be quite used to seeing someone like James Bond arriving in a speed boat and jumping off it to drink a Martini cocktail, shaken, not stirred, with them.

"Neither. By bike. See you later!"

That's good. Well, at least they're open tonight, and it's not fully booked. It's now mid-afternoon as I turn back over the Ringling Causeway from Sarasota and up along the beautiful Gulf of Mexico Drive to the Sandpiper Inn. I'm astounded when I arrive. There's now one car parked up. I place the bike under the only bit of shade and walk back to my seafront paradise.

Within a few minutes, I'm feeling the warm sand between my toes again and soaking up the rays. Seeing what I've now seen, these fabulous barrier island beaches are definitely the best places to stay. I can't believe that I'll already be leaving this place tomorrow to get back to Lake Wales and getting ready for the Orlando show the day after that. Time is flying by, and I can't hold it back. That's the amazing and sometimes frustrating thing in life. Time whizzes by when you're enjoying yourself and feeling fulfilled, but, when you're not, time just doesn't seem to move and goes by tortuously slowly.

This sentiment unfortunately brings to the surface what I've been trying to avoid and think about. It reminds me only too vividly about the unhappy, stressful, and sometimes "thumb twiddling, have-to-make-myself-look-busy" office job I'm currently in. I'm not happy. Period. I have palpitations every day I walk into that place. But the dilemma is I don't know what I want to go on and do for a better, more rewarding and less stressful life. I'll have to make a decision before it kills me. At least that's one good thing about me; I may be spontaneous and make decisions quickly, but I also then act on them. Maybe when I get back I should just try and put some money away, so, if I can't handle it anymore and need to jump ship before finding something, I'll at least have some back up for a short while until I figure out what I can do. That makes me feel a little better, but, with no concrete strategy, I'll have to figure that one out when I get back.

Just as the sun is setting, I get back on the bike and do the couple of miles down to the little Mobile gas station and turn down a small lane to a big boat yard. It's there I also see a small staircase opposite with signs up to "The Grill."

I park up next to the wall, lock the helmet carefully onto the handlebars on the side of the wall and out of prying eyes, and take my bag and money out from the side panniers. But this time, as it's a smart place, I take my comb out and smooth my hair down, wrap a shawl round me, and change from my boots to sandals. I walk over to peer into the boathouse. The covered warehouse is enormous, but what's amazing are the hundreds of boats suspended in layers ready, no doubt, to get out onto the water at any time.

Outside on the jetty are more boats suspended out from the water. The tall palm trees in front of them are starting to blow with the wind that's picked up slightly, but, on this side of the key, facing the bay, the water is calm, with no waves and just slight rippling up to the jetties. Out in the distance, across the bay, I see the city of Sarasota and notice the first lights coming on. I walk back and up the small metal staircase of the red brick building and enter a fabulous, darkly lit bar with giant fish and surf boards hanging from the walls. There's even a massive shark hanging from the ceiling. I see other people arriving, and it's already looking fairly busy, with waiters busily carrying trays of food and drink.

A girl smiles and greets me. "Welcome to the Dry Dock Grill. Do you wish to eat here inside, or outside on the dock?"

I smile, "I'd love to eat outside, if that's OK."

"That's fine. We're currently going to have people leaving in the next ten to fifteen minutes, so why don't I get you a drink from the bar?"

Now that would be good. I don't normally ever drink when riding, but, surely, I can afford to have just one beer. I surrender. The chilled beer arrives, and, perched on a stool, I pick up a copy of the Longboat Key News newspaper and flip through it. Nothing much seems to happen here of any great gravity besides golf tournaments, tennis matches, art auctions, and openings of new restaurants. Maybe I'm exaggerating slightly, but it does seem like it's all hunky dory here.

My number is shortly called, and I'm led out to a table outside overlooking Sarasota Bay. Out in front of me is an emerald green boat hanging in the air, in front of a soft pink horizon merging perfectly into a scarlet blue sky, which is getting progressively darker the further up I look, until the sky above me is pitch dark with the stars coming out over the water.

I sip my beer, and a girl comes over with a lighter for the night light on the table so I can read the menu. "Our specials tonight are the lobster bisque, and we also have fresh sea scallops, and, of course, we're serving the grouper sandwich, which is renowned as the best on Florida's west coast!"

Leaning towards the little flame and squinting my eyes, I can just about read the menu. I quickly opt for the half dozen freshly shucked raw seasonal oysters sourced from around here in the Gulf and, what else, but their famous grouper sandwich—a thick flaky grouper filet, blackened, and served on a soft roll, with a side of French fries and a sweet chilli and cilantro sauce. I'm far from disappointed. It's a gastronomic delight, full of freshness and taste of the sea.

The atmosphere is magical, but, before long, I'm putting my helmet on, once again, and carefully riding back in the dark. But, with the nice thought that when I get back I still have some good wine left to drink out under the star-studded sky, I feel that days like this should never end.

12

GARDEN GHOSTS

Longboat Key, Florida, to Lake Wales, Florida

114 miles

The natural light flows through the seaside window shutters and ripples over the bed and onto my face. I stretch my arms and hoist myself out, walking out onto the sunny terrace and breathing in the fresh, salty air and see the waves crashing onto the beach.

So what's the plan of action today Zoë? And what do we need to do? Well, I reckon it's going to be a pretty easy one. I'll ride back later this morning to Lake Wales and then, no doubt, get instructed by Mike on what the plan is for the next couple of days when we're going to have to bike it up to Orlando every day for the show. I hear Orlando's a pretty non-stop busy place, never sleeping, with buckets of tourists coming to the theme park attractions and Disney World, so it certainly won't be leisurely rides there and back.

The idea of commuting at rush hour there and back on heavy congested roads doesn't seem too appealing, but I'm sure we'll survive. If I'm following Mike, at least to start with, then that'll definitely be easier on the stress levels and no excuse to get lost. I'm sure it will be fun. It's all going to be new, so that's good.

But at the moment, I want to live for the present and enjoy for just a few more hours this lovely place. I open the fridge door to see it's pretty empty, with nothing very appetizing to eat for breakfast besides a bit of paté and dry bread. That I'll give a miss. The idea of popping over the road to The Blue Dolphin Cafe for a nice American breakfast sounds a lot more appealing.

I wander out to the roadside, passing and kicking the tyres of the bike. Nothing's broken, missing, or deflated. I cross the empty road and walk over to what I can only describe as a typical little American shopping outlet with a row of quaint, practical shops and cafes lined side by side, with a giant car park just in front. There's your Mama's Household Kitchen Supplies Shop, the Gift & Postcard Store, a hairdressers, courier service agency, a typical Tex-Mex eaterie, and, in the middle of it all, The Blue Dolphin, which I'd been told at the hotel serves "generous helpings of tasty food."

Approaching it, I amusingly see a couple of generous sized people walking in. They kindly smile and hold the door open for me. I walk in. All around the walls of this large room are surfboards and fun beachy décor and a big, long breakfast bar up by the kitchens. There are already plenty of people sitting at the tables heartily digging into big breakfasts. I decide to go and sit on a stool at the bar and watch a bit of the action.

I love these sorts of places. The service is always good, and, due to the simplicity of their dishes, you normally don't get too surprised in what you can order.

The girl behind the counter has noticed me and smiles, handing me a massive menu while pouring me a glass of chilled water. "Morning. Can I get you a coffee?"

I nod, and, with that, she promptly picks up a jug from the other end of the counter and pours me a coffee into a big mug with a dolphin on it. She slides down the counter a jug of milk and a bowl of sugar to me. I smile in gratitude. There's everything here on the menu from fajita wraps, Caesar salad, "Surfer Burger", and hot dogs, but that's not quite what tempts me for the first meal of the day. Then I pick up yet another menu with their "Breakfast Specials." This looks better. I'll go for the "Waffle Works" with fresh strawberries, bananas, and blueberries. It probably isn't, but at least it sounds a bit healthy.

Wiping my mouth with the paper towel, I look at an almost empty plate, give or take a few blueberries. God, that was massive but good! I'm convincing myself not to feel guilty and that maybe I won't know where I'll be for lunch and may not be able to find any food. That seems like a pretty ridiculous and feeble excuse, considering where I am—the land of food and consumption.

My memory is suddenly jolted. There is one thing I want to try to find before leaving, and this seems like a good place, as I've been told it's pretty good for shopping.

I know it's incredible to believe, but, back in the UK, I actually have an American king size bed, which I'd shipped over when I moved back. Now, the problem is I just can't get the sheets big enough for it over there. There'll come a day when I've got to get rid of it, as it just doesn't fit in most standard rooms over there, but, at the moment, I just need more sheets. I wonder if there's anywhere nearby. I looked on Lido Key when walking round St. Armands Circle yesterday, but nothing. I'll ask the couple in dressing gowns back at the hotel.

I knock politely on the door and hear the predictable barking behind it. It's the lady this time, with large rollers in her hair, who greets me. "Good morning. Did you have a good stay? We'll need to ask you to leave by eleven AM so we can clean the room. I'll get your bill ready for when you vacate it."

"Thanks. Yes, it's been great," I reply honestly. "I know this sounds like a silly question, but would you know a place I could go to on the way back that sells bed sheets, and big ones at that?"

The lady pushes one of her rollers back into place and thinks for a moment. "Well, if you're heading back to Bradenton, I do know there's a pretty big "Bed, Bath & Beyond" on the retail strip along Cortez Road. Do you know where I mean?"

To be honest, I obviously don't, but say politely, "Well, not really, as it's the first time I've been here. But if it's going to be really difficult to find, I may not bother."

"I promise you. You can't go wrong." I think I've heard that one before!

"All you need do is cross over the first bridge when you get to Bradenton Beach and just continue for a few miles along Cortez Road."

I thank her and, just to make sure, which I've found is always wise, find the number and give the store a call to make sure they're still there, open, and that they stock what I'm looking for. It's all affirmative. So, hopefully, that one's sorted.

I reluctantly pack my stuff up, but not before walking back out onto the beach one last time and sitting down on one of the recliners. The sandpipers are out in force this morning, running in and out from the water's edge in strategic merriment—quite a mesmerizing sight. Before I know it, another half hour has slipped away, and I really need to vacate the room.

I turn the water tap on at the beach and wash my feet clean and salt-free, then put on my socks and boots. I go through the garden down to the reception, get my card swiped, and then, with my bag and helmet, walk over to the bike and secure everything down.

The bike purrs into action, and, signalling left, I cross and turn back up Longboat Key. With the warmth surrounding me, almost like a protective cocoon, I make sure to ride extra slowly to absorb and enjoy every last moment of this beautiful place.

I'm soon, within a blink of an eye, over Longboat Pass and riding along Bradenton Beach, seeing people promenading up and down and simply enjoying the day. My concentration has slipped for a second. I need to look out for where I need to turn. Luckily, it's at that very moment that I spot the junction and the road I need to turn onto to get over Anna Maria Sound and onto the 684, or Cortez Road, in Bradenton. I very quickly signal right and slip onto the new road riding over the large waterway.

Now I am surprised. This is one hell of a busy, long road, full of industrial sites, garages, commercial outlets, and like nothing from the exquisite historic area I'd seen in the north of the town just a few days earlier. It's going to be difficult to stop with all this traffic. I'm needing to concentrate and find number 825 Cortez Road West. Stopping at one of the many traffic lights, the numbers seem to be in their thousands, so I'm probably still quite a distance from where I need to be. With no sat-nav, I'm totally dependent on the address I've written down and by just looking out for the numbers on the buildings.

A few miles farther down, I'm getting concerned that I haven't seen anything remotely looking like a bed store in any of these retail outlets. And it's then that I approach a massive intersection leading me out of the town! I've somehow gone wrong, but, strangely, couldn't find the number on this road. There's now masses of traffic from behind pushing me to go on, and with nowhere to really stop and double check. But I'm not going to give up. I need those sheets. So I go back round from the intersection and return along the same road, but in the opposite direction, now seeing the numbers going up. All of a sudden, on the other side of the road, inside a monster retail outlet, I see the small word *Bed*. I quickly signal and cross over, parking up outside the store. I've made it.

The shopping experience is an easy one; right colour, right size, and I'm out! I tie the sheets down onto the back seat. Maybe not your typical souvenir, but very useful.

I turn left, up through the busy city and somehow find and get onto Florida Route 64 East. I sigh with just a little bit of relief and know there really isn't anything much to worry about now in getting back. This road I know, and I also know it should get me all the way back to Avon Park. So, for about seventy idyllic miles, I'm riding back through the swamplands, forests, and farmlands of this lesser known part of western Florida that most people from out of town would bypass. For the ease of speed and directness they'd use all the nearby major highways. Not me! I'm glad I took Mike's advice and ignored my initial idea of heading towards St. Petersburg.

It's definitely a place I'd go back to, feeling I need to spend more time exploring Sarasota, even going to its famous racetrack and that beach on Siesta Key.

I go over some railway lines on this quiet road, which I now know leads me into Avon Park, down the main street and back onto US Route 27 northbound to Lake Wales. It's only a comparatively short trip, but it feels, to me, like a big accomplishment.

Before I know it, Lake Wales beckons me, and I come off the highway. Approaching the intersection, I look down again at Mike's little hand drawn map, that I'd swapped over from the large one in Avon Park, and see the lake with the McDonalds opposite, just on my right. We're here!

Riding over the tracks on Central Avenue and coming towards the lake with the residential homes, I'm noticing that things have changed since I've been away. I'm noticing pumpkins of all sizes on the door steps and gooley orange and black decorations hanging on the windows and walls. Well, of course, we're just a few weeks away from Halloween, on the last day of October. Here in America, it seems to be taken a lot more seriously, with homes extensively decorated and a much longer lead up time, unlike in Britain.

Hoping there's some food in the fridge to make a sandwich when I get back, I recognise the purple painted colonial house on the corner and happily turn along Lakeshore Drive, knowing I'm almost back. It's there that I go past a very normal looking, small white home, but what's outside and in front of it certainly isn't! I'm so astounded by what I see and the enormity of it, that I need to stop and do a double take.

Out at the front has to be at least fifty grave stones standing, leaning, or fallen on the grass, with what look like skulls and skeletons lying next to and in between them. There's other interesting stuff, so I feel it's something maybe Mike and the kids would appreciate seeing in more detail. I'll let them know when I get back.

I turn up past the playing fields and see Jacob walking along the street with a back pack on and carrying a baseball bat. He hears me, or rather the bike, coming and turns round smiling.

I park up in the driveway and turn the engine off. Pulling my helmet off, I see Jacob's been joined by his sister, Tess. They walk up curiously.

"So, how was it? Did you see some sea?"

"I sure did and even got my feet wet!"

They laugh, and I see Mike walking out of the garage with a cloth in his hand. "Hey! The wanderer has returned. How was it over at Longboat? Did you like it?"

"It was fantastic. Just what I'd been looking for, and I'll certainly go by your recommendations in the future. The bike went well, and those directions along 64 were perfect.

Didn't get lost once, except for when I was looking for sheets!"

Their eyes all widen in surprise.

"Ah, just sheets to take home that I can't buy over there. Anyway, more importantly, what are you guys doing? I've just got to show you something I've just gone past up the road."

The kids look curiously at me while I continue explaining, "There's a house up there with the most incredible graveyard. Have you seen it?"

Tess eagerly says with pleading eyes, "Oh, Dad. That house is always good. Can we go? Please? It sounds scary!"

Mike smiles. "Sure, and, while we're at it, we can go grab a sandwich in town and show the wanderer around a bit more. Zoë, you go and drop your stuff off and we'll see you here in five."

"OK, maybe six, after I've washed my face and hands and tidied up a bit with a clean T-shirt and flip-flops!"

We all walk over to the house on Lakeshore and stop outside, with the kids mouths wide open. The grassy frontage has been transformed into a spooky graveyard, and each headstone seems to have something engraved or painted on it. Bones, skulls, mummies, and skeletons are dispersed among them.

"Come on, Mike. You're one for adventure. Let's go up to the house and introduce ourselves and see if we can walk around to get a better look."

The kids clap their hands in agreement. So we wander up the long pathway to the porch, where there's an inflated witch and cauldron, a giant inflated black cat, and a black ghost hanging from the balcony. We politely knock on the door. After a while, an old lady peers through the glass and slowly opens the door. I'm imagining her to be dressed like a witch, which, unfortunately, she isn't.

I take the lead with my accent. "Afternoon, Ma'am. We were walking by and couldn't help but notice your gravestones. It's incredible here. Would it be possible to wander round and have a proper look? So much work has been done!"

She smiles. "Sure. My kids and grandchildren have done this. Go take a look. There's lots to see."

We thank her and take a wander. It's like a miniature theme park! We start giggling when we see what's written on some of the tombstones: "M. T. Tomb", "Dee Cayed", "Carry M. Off", "Hammond Eggs", "Do Not Disturb", "Manny Bones", "I. M. Saved". Around the garden are some big trees with Spanish Moss hanging down, and also hanging from them are ghost-like white sheets, and there's an open coffin leaning against one of the tree trunks. It looks like it would be even scarier at night, as we notice hidden lights intertwined in the trees.

We wave and thank the kind lady goodbye and wander a couple of blocks into the deserted town, where there seems to be nobody but us. We approach a little cafe and go out onto the terrace, eating chicken sandwiches and looking out at the empty street.

I state the obvious, "It seems real quiet around here."

"Yea, it's what we like. But this place used to be raucous during the '20s when it developed and grew during our Great Florida Land Boom. Before that, Lake Wales had only been found about ten years earlier in 1911 by a group of business men who purchased 5,000 acres in this hilly wilderness around our Lake Wailes. Those guys were wise, as they thought the pine forests would form the basis of the turpentine and timber industry, the sandy soil would be ideal for growing oranges, lemons, and other citrus fruit, and these rolling hills would be perfect for a town.

Looking over between the red bricked buildings, I see something totally out of context and which I'd noticed briefly when I first arrived. Closer up, it's pretty impressive. It's a tall "skyscraper" looking white building, that looks like it's been empty and unused for a long, long time.

I point over, "What's that?"

Swallowing the last mouthful of his sandwich. Mike continues. "Ah, that place has history and a story. It's the Grand Hotel. That, too, was built during the boom in the '20s and is one of the few remaining skyscrapers built in Florida during that time. They say, even at that time, it cost about half a million dollars but, unfortunately, opened just as the boom began to crash. It stands there as part of our history here.

"If we had more time we could also have taken you to Bok Tower, on Iron Mountain, which is another historic landmark here built around the 1920s, too. The tower has fifty-seven bells, which ring out and you can hear them a long way away. It's on our highest point of peninsular Florida, about three hundred feet above sea level, and there's a wildlife sanctuary and lots of beautiful landscaped gardens at its feet. Never enough time. Come on kids, eat up, we've gotta get back, and you've got to do your homework!"

The kids sigh, "Oh, do we really have to?"

We get up to leave and wander back to the house, which, itself, is one of the oldest in the town. Walking through the quiet residential streets, we wander past trees with massive amounts of beautiful Spanish moss hanging from every branch and almost touching the grass below.

I notice Mike winking at Tess, then walking over behind the hanging moss. He drapes some of the moss over his face making it look like he's got an enormous white moustache and beard down to his waist. We all laugh out loud and try it for ourselves. It's sometimes the simplest and silliest things which create the biggest laughs.

So, still giggling, we walk back to the house, but before we're there the kids enthusiastically shout out, "We know, Zoë! We can do more fun stuff when we get back and go into the back yard. We have a line between the trees that you can hang onto and slide all the way down to the end of the yard. It's fast and a lot of fun. Do you wanna go?"

I smile "Yes, why not? As long as I don't break anything!"

So, precariously standing on a step ladder that the kids are holding, I grab the handles on the overhead carriage, and they remove the ladder away and push me away, and off I go, whizzing down to the bottom of the garden with my feet in the air, jumping off just in time at the end. Fun. By now, the kids have chased and caught up with me and run back with the carriage to do it themselves.

Mike walks out from his woodshop, "You'd never know it now but we had to almost totally rebuild the house about ten years ago. The roof was ripped off."

I look at him in astonishment and disbelief.

He continues, "In 2004, Lakes Wales endured three massive hurricanes, which came though this area. There was Hurricane Charley, Hurricane Frances, and Hurricane Jeanne. And you know what? They damn well all arrived within just over a month. One night the roof above the veranda across the front of the house was just blown off by the wind. We knew the storm was coming but had nowhere to go. We just had to hide in the closet in the bedroom hoping all would be well. The place is beautiful, and that's why we live here, but hurricanes—you never quite know when the next one will come to potentially destroy people's homes and lives."

There's not a lot I can add to that. Mike continues in a more light hearted way, "And tomorrow is another day, with no hurricanes predicted. But we'll have a busy day. The show starts around ten, and it'll take us at least an hour to get there on the bikes if the roads aren't congested, with no filtering here, and that's before we've even registered. I also think we'll have to be shuttled from where we park the bikes. If we leave around eight'ish that should give us plenty of time. Let's wheel the bikes in, then you can unpack and tell us all about what you discovered and did at Longboat."

The kids clap enthusiastically and sit down ready to hear another story, which I'll try hard to make funny.

13

LOST ON THE HIGHWAY!

Lake Wales, Florida, to Orlando, Florida, and back to Lakes Wales

About 88 miles

I'm feeling just a little bit jittery and nervous about not really knowing what to expect when we arrive at the show in Orlando, knowing I'll need to get access to it and then meet up with the guys from RokStraps to plan our day. It had, I guess, all been done a bit at the last minute, when I'd contacted them out of the blue. They'd, surprisingly, welcomed the idea of me joining them to book sign.

When I see Mike's smiling face, while he's making the coffee in the kitchen and handing me a mug, I somehow feel things will be fine.

"I was listening on the radio that we're gonna have to be pretty patient on the bikes this morning. As soon as we get off US 27 onto I-4 to Orlando, that's where we'll hit the traffic. Plus the Convention Center is just past all the theme parks. You know—Disney, Epcot, SeaWorld. So we'll have congestion from that, too."

I nod and show my concern. "I guess it's only normal there. But, to be honest with you, I'm not really looking forward to negotiating these traffic-laden, busy roads. I feel that recently we've had more than a bit of luxury in avoiding them."

Mike replies matter of factly, "Well, we gotta get there and it's the only practical way. I've gotta be with the guys from the VJMC. You know, the guys we met over in Alabama. You're also gonna have to sweet talk your way into the show and try and get a press pass; I've already got mine; then see your guys at Rok Straps to sort out the book stuff. Before you got back yesterday, we transported the boxes of books up and they're under some tables on the VJMC bike show area. I guess the day is gonna be pretty frantic for me, and I've got a drinks reception with my guys in the evening, so you may just want to head back here to Lake Wales on your own."

I look a little surprised, having not planned for that possibility, and feel just slightly concerned by this new revelation. "On my own!"

"Don't worry, Zoë. I'll draw you one of my famous maps, and I'm sure with that you'll be able to find your way back."

Having never taken this route into metropolitan Orlando, I'm going to have to be extra meticulous in remembering the way up and make note of all the possible landmarks, which will reassure me I'm coming back on the same roads. I know this sounds pathetic, but I'm going to make sure I also leave well before it gets dark. There's no way, in a month of Sundays, that I'm going to try and navigate busy, unknown roads on my own in the dark. I'll probably end up somewhere not even on the map!

All it takes is one wrong turn, and I may be forced to ride for miles and miles before I can turn off, and then what? As usual, I'm starting to worry before anything has even happened.

I breathe deeply. "Alright, Mike, if you say so. But I'll probably, in that case, make my way back before the event closes so I'm not navigating back in the dark."

He nods, understanding my concern. "Yea. Good idea. and you should then be able to avoid the rush hour traffic. Though, without worrying you, I do have to say that it's always busy south of the city with those theme parks and all the hotels out on International Drive. Keep close behind me this morning and make sure you see when I'm indicating. We don't want to lose you already."

We roll the bikes out from the garage and have the luxury of not tying any heavy bags down on the seats. Once again, Mike puts on his heavy bike jacket, gets on, and looks behind to make sure that I'm ready to follow.

We start both Bonnies and head out on the now familiar road, past the baseball pitches, along the lakeside, over the railway tracks, past McDonalds, and quickly head northwards on US Route 27.

This part of the highway is still relatively quiet and pretty nice to ride on. But shortly, before I know it, and close to Dundee, Mike has sighted something and is indicating to get off it already.

He looks over to me as if to also say I should be doing the same. "Gas here should be cheaper than when we hit Orlando."

So I obediently follow suit, fill my tank up for about eight dollars and also grab a bottle of water, which I take a gulp from then stuff back into my side bag.

Back out on the road, I'm starting to see more and more traffic, and even Mike is starting to get impatient with some of the slower drivers hogging the middle lane, so he starts more and more to quickly overtake them with me frantically trying to keep up. I feel like we've notched up a gear or two in speed and urgency. It's not until we reach the major intersection and jump onto Interstate Route 4 northbound, and continuing for about another twenty miles, that I'm starting to understand what he'd said about the traffic density going into Orlando. This isn't fun. There's lots of it, and, in the hot sun, I'm concentrating madly to keep sight of Mike between the camper vans, trucks, and cars, not knowing quite when we'll be exiting.

This mayhem seems to go on for quite a while until I start seeing signs for the Walt Disney World Resort and the Epcot Center. Just as we hit the signs for SeaWorld, I notice Mike looking into his mirrors and then signalling well in advance to give me enough time to veer into the inner lane to get off at Exit 72. Then it's down Florida Route 528 and off onto famous International Drive, running parallel to Interstate 4, where signs for the Orange County Convention Center quickly confirm its proximity. International Drive is really Orlando's tourist hub, packed with masses of restaurant chains, bars, shops, hotels, motels, and inns and close to the many theme parks. This is sometimes the only place visitors to Orlando get to see.

Getting closer to the conventon center, the road becomes divided, with palm trees on either side. We somehow, and not intentionally, ride past the large front entrance of the convention center, where I positively think we'll be simply able to just park up. But that's a dream. There's no parking but just a good clue. With true American style and service, we see a multitude of shuttle buses ferrying people back and forth from a multitude of car parks. We then notice a small road sign indicating where we need to go and park our bikes in the special area reserved for them. So we follow a shuttle bus and arrive at what I can only describe as a humungous outdoor parking area, just for the motorbikes. There are already hundreds and hundreds parked in rows as far as the eye can see.

I watch Mike slow down and look around, sussing it out as he enters. He's obviously looking to see where there's room for us to best stop and park up. Perfect. A place near the edge of the parking area, close to the shuttle buses, and, incredibly, in some shade. We'll need to manoeuvre the bikes a bit! We squeeze between two other bikes, a large Victory and a Harley, and pack away gloves and stuff we don't need to take with us.

Mike takes his helmet off and tightens the elastic band round his pony tail. "Boy this place is another world. Not my kind of world, and already busy like hell. Look at all those people lining up for the bus to get a ride back to the convention center. Oh well, let's be like cattle too and go join them and try not to swelter too much from the heat."

We walk over to the shuttle bus stop, and, thankfully, within just a few minutes, with American efficiency, we're whizzed off to the convention center entrance, with big signs overhead for "AIMEXPO", the American International Motorcycle Expo.

We go up the escalators, walk over the thick, velvety carpet, and look around for signs on where to go to exactly.

Mike starts pointing, "Look over there. That's the registration area. Try and sweet talk them with your English accent for a press pass. Shouldn't be a problem. You can say you're with me and spending time on the RokStraps booth. That pass will also give you food and drink in the press area all day."

He sounds very confident, but it's not him having to do what I'm going to have to do. I breathe in deeply and walk confidently up to the desk with the row of people behind it and look seriously at the kindest looking one of them. "Morning. I've come in from London and need a press pass. I'm working with a local publisher here in Florida."

She looks quizzically at me to decipher whether I'm lying, with no real ID to show her. I stand my ground. About half an hour later, after speaking with numerous people, I put the press pass over my head and walk smiling over to Mike, who must now be drinking his third coffee.

He's engrossed in reading something and suddenly looks up. "It's looking pretty impressive from what I've read here in their show directory. It only started here last year, in 2013, and they've already got 500 exhibitors and are saying it's going to become the most important show for motorcycling and power sports in North America.

"Now remember, Zoë", you go and have a wander to orientate yourself. I'll head over to the VJMC and Retro Affair Bike Show area to get situated. Go and introduce yourself to your guys, then come back over, and we can take the books over to them."

We show our passes and walk onto the exhibition floor. There are already lots of people walking up and down the aisles looking curiously at everything going on, with music blaring from speakers and lightly clad hostesses beckoning people with gleaming white smiles to come and visit them at their booths. I stop and look down at the floor plan I'd been given and identify where I need to go. I walk down one of the aisles and see two cheery-faced guys standing by the RokStraps booth chatting away to a couple of people carrying helmets.

I wait until they're finished, then walk over "Hey, are you Rich and Gary? I'm Zoë."

They both nod simultaneously "We sure are!' says one of them with an Aussie accent "I'm Gary, and that's Rich. We were looking forward to meeting you and getting you set up here with us. We're more than happy for you to spend a couple of hours today and tomorrow at our booth. That should attract some people over here, which is always a good thing."

What a great welcome, and so generous. "That's great, guys. Mike's gonna come back with me with the books, so we'll see you here a bit later on."

"Not a problem, and we wanna hear all about what you've been doing while you've been over here in America."

I smile, happy they're happy. "Absolutely. I'm sure we'll have plenty of time this afternoon."

We shake hands again, and I rush back to where Mike said he'd be. I arrive and see him sitting behind a long set of tables, and all around are beautiful vintage and classic Japanese bikes.

He sees me approaching. "So, how you like these bikes? Looking good aren't they? Have my Honda on display here this year. And guess who just walked over, and you've just missed. Mark and Steve, from Ace Cafe USA. They said you'd better pop over and see them. They'd mentioned about a bike run and invite for a press launch at their downtown Orlando site tomorrow morning. Why don't you go and get some details. Sounds like fun."

I wander over to the Ace Cafe booth area and see Mark chatting away. He sees me from the corner of his eye and puts his finger up indicating I wait for a second.

He then walks over, smiling from cheek to cheek. "Hey, Zoë. Good to see you. Hope the ride back from Birmingham was good. Saw Mike and told him what we'd chatted about at Barber. We'd love to see you guys at our little gathering at the building site tomorrow morning. There'll be some press and local people who're involved in the project.

"We'll have breakfast there and some pictures and plans on what the Ace Cafe USA is gonna look like. Don't forget it's just an empty building at the moment. It's on West Livingston Street, number 100. You'll see it's an old iconic, but derelict, music venue and church that hasn't been used for years. It's only about ten minutes from here, so you'll be able to quickly get back to the show afterward."

I smile, nodding. "Sounds really interesting, and we'd love to come. We'll be biking up from Lake Wales, which is about an hour away, so we'll come over directly. See you then!"

Like true pros, Mike and I arrive punctually at two PM at the RokStraps booth, laden with books, big smiles, and bags of British chocolate for them. We're greeted like long, lost family, and, for the next couple hours, I'm talking ten to the dozen with people fascinated to hear all about my stories. People are also excited to be talking about their own travels and plans. One incredible couple, Carol and Ken Duval, originally from Brisbane, Australia, are literally spending their lives on bikes, travelling around the world. And their journey doesn't seem to be coming to an end!

Towards the end of the afternoon, I see Mike wandering back to have what looks like a serious chat. "So. how's it going? The show's going to be over in an hour, and then I'm going over for the drinks reception. Now's probably a good time for you to start making a move to get your bike and head out."

I nod in eager agreement, already feeling I need a plan travelling back on my own for the first time. "Yes. I agree. And, to tell you the truth, I think by the time I get the shuttle back to the bike parking, find it, sort myself out, have it clear in my head on how to get out of here, and get onto the right road it'll already be about five o'clock. Then the traffic will, I'm sure, be already starting to build up. If it's anything to go by from this morning, it's going to be busy and particularly nasty past the parks. The key for me is not to bike out in the dark, or I won't be able to read the directions, and I'll panic. Knowing me, I'll get lost!"

Rich and Gary look at me, nodding in sympathy, but Mike reassures me that as far as he's concerned everything will be fine. "Just don't worry, Zoë. Go back the way we came, past the theme parks, but go further than you think before jumping back onto US Route 27 homebound. I'll be leaving in a couple of hours, myself, so we can all eat together when I get back."

So I say goodbye to the boys and walk back with Mike to collect my helmet. I get out into the blistering afternoon sunshine and jump into an air-conditioned shuttle bus crowded with people holding carrier bags full of exhibition souvenirs, leaflets, and maybe some nice, new biking gear. The bus stops outside the outdoor Action Area, where bikes have been demonstrated and stunts performed all day. I walk back over the large expanse of parking space, literally filled with thousands of bikes, until I finally locate my little bike, still squashed between its new friends, the Victory and Harley. No damage to it, so all's well.

In reality, I don't really have the first clue on how to navigate out of here and then get back onto the right road and, just as importantly, in the right direction. I can feel a few palpitations starting.

I strap my helmet on and pull the sun visor down. I tentatively start up, slide out from between the two bikes, and slowly navigate through the rows of bikes to the exit point, where I see a guard by the gates. I'm not proud. "Never refuse an opportunity to ask." That should be my motto.

I pull my visor up and smile. "Hi. I'm just checking the best way to get onto 528 West."

The guard also smiles. "You're certainly from out of town, from what I can hear. If you go eastbound it'll be wrong, it'll take you over to Cape Canaveral. So look out for westbound signs getting out of here. Make sure to keep in your middle lane, just to be sure. Look out for signs for Disney"

That's it. If there's ever a problem, look out for Disney! Mickey will help you. That's what I'll do. I cautiously head out, palpitating a little that I'm now out on the big roads on my own and with quite a bit of navigation to do. Once I've accelerated out onto the main highways, I'll have very little opportunity to stop and pull over to take a better look at Mike's hand drawn map and the bigger map of Florida underneath it.

Exiting the venue, joy of joys, this is too easy! I hit 528 West and, with the hot breeze rushing past me, jump onto Interstate 4 and, obviously, southbound. But far too soon, the traffic has already come to a complete stand still as I approach Disney, and I'm feeling very vulnerable, sitting on the bike in the middle of traffic in the sweltering heat. Again, if this was back in Britain you wouldn't have seen me for dust. I'd have gone through the traffic without hesitation.

It's got to be about twenty minutes before the traffic slowly starts to move again, and then, just like magic, it all disappears and the road is once again flowing smoothly. But I'm already anxious. I know I have to look out for exit signs to get me onto US 27 South, but I already feel like I've gone too far. At least the bike is running well, there's fuel in it, and I'm not sensing there'll be any immediate problems.

I continue looking up at the signs and bizarrely feel I don't recognise them. Have I, in the mayhem of the traffic, maybe gone past my exit junction? My mind is now racing. Where would I now be able to get off, and how would I get back to find the right road again? I'm panicking, unable to stop to clearly look at the map. I need some reassurance that I just need to stick on this road. Should I get off it? Should I stay on it? I need some signs. I decide to keep going and, about ten miles farther on, see the wonderful number 27! Route 27 will now lead me all the way back to Lake Wales, and, on this road, I can just relax and enjoy the ride back.

I go around, up, and over the highway onto 27. I feel so happy I'll stop somewhere and treat myself to a cold drink. 27 is a good road, with junctions and traffic lights and interesting farm stalls and commercial outlets, so it won't be a problem.

I soon see the perfect place that has everything: a gas station, next to that a coffee shop, and next to that, and perhaps even better, a Western boot shop. Now, that is tempting and all on my side of the road.

I turn off and park right outside the store with the enormous big red cowboy boot next to the doorway. Curiosity gets the better of me. I walk inside. Shelves and all the available floor space are packed full to the beams with boots of every size, colour, and description. On one of the shelves is a very "eye pleasing" pair of handcrafted, black leather Old Gringo boots with short Cuban heels. Unfortunately, their size is too big, like their price tag!

I walk back out and, quickly sweating from the heat, rush into the coffee shop and grab a cold SevenUp from the fridge and a bag of potato chips. Which reminds me; I didn't really get much of a chance to eat that much back at the show, besides a sandwich in the press lounge. Hopefully Mike won't get back that late, and Andrea will be back from work, so we can all eat dinner together. I finish the drink and bag of chips and ride the short distance over to the gas station. I'll top up now, which will avoid me having to do it tomorrow morning.

With all that done, I pop back onto 27 and enjoy the last twenty miles of stressless biking, now knowing exactly where I'm going and that I'll get back in the light. A nice glass of chilled wine when I get back, out on the porch, will be perfect. But, if my memory serves me well, I didn't recall seeing any in the fridge—just beers. I'll keep an eye out for something on the road.

As luck would have it, just before entering Lake Wales, I see on the other side of the road ABC Fine Wine & Spirits. I

Perfect. I cross over the road, park up, as you always can do in America, just outside the front door, and walk into a wine lover's paradise. Bottles of all ages and from all areas of the country and the world are there. I start chatting with a friendly guy, and he's soon persuaded me to get a "really good" Californian. I'll take two!

I walk over to pay and notice something behind the counter, which takes my breath away. A life-size, crystal glass bottle, in the shape of a human skull, full of vodka. God, that would be a good party piece! I ask to have a closer look at it, but the skull is massively heavy. Firstly, it wouldn't fit in my side bags and, secondly, it would probably get emptied by us before getting back to London. A little disappointed, I pay for the wines but notice hand size skulls of the same vodka. No question, due to their quirkiness, I'll take two for presents. One for Paul, my good friend back in London who loves the stuff, and one for my niece, Chloë, who, like any student, can't resist the odd drop of vodka from time to time.

A few hours later, we're all back and sitting outside in the backyard, having already been tempted to decapitate one of the vodka heads.

14

ACE OF A DAY!

Lake Wales, Florida, to Downtown Orlando, Florida, and back

95 miles

Something suddenly wakes me up. I'm sure I can hear the sound of a bike starting and revving up outside the house. I hope I haven't overslept! I lean down and fumble for the watch on the floor and see it's only just after seven. Surely, Mike's not ready to go yet.

My brain starts racing. Maybe he's wanting to beat that "traffic from hell' congestion into Orlando or, probably more truthfully, to give himself more time to find the place. I remember him saying that he didn't really know where we needed to get to exactly for the Ace breakfast invite, which, apparently, was somewhere in downtown Orlando, the historic core and central business district.

I curiously peer out of the window and can see Mike tinkering away with his bike out at the front and, once again, stuffing things into his panniers.

I push the window open, "Hey, Mike, how you doing? Nice alarm clock!"

"Morning, Zoë. Sorry. Just checking. Had some suspicion coming back last night in the dark that the rear suspension wasn't as firm as it should be. It looks like I needed to pump the tyres up. I've done that already inside the garage, and all seems fine now."

Wiping his hands down his trousers, he adds, "No rush, but need to leave in about thirty minutes!"

He makes me smile. No rush. Right! But just be ready pretty quick. I also smile discreetly to myself, as I've noticed that Mike might just be wearing a brightly coloured rock 'n' roll looking scarf around his neck, that I've never seen before, to maybe blend in with the guys when we get to The Ace later.

A few minutes later we're both seated at the kitchen table, drinking coffee and looking at the Orlando street maps.

Mike nods to himself, looking like he's got a plan. "Yea. If I got it right, although the streets up there look like spaghetti loops, we just need to head past our normal Exit 72 at the convention center, continue up on lovely, busy Interstate 4, past Wet 'n' Wild, Harry Potter's Place, and the Universal Resort and get off at Exit 83. Then I think we drive through some of the business district, which shouldn't be too busy with it being Saturday and then West Livingston Street should be just in front of us. Well, that's how I see it."

He's said all that without even taking a gasp. I simply nod in agreement, hoping he really does know where we're going, because I sure as hell don't.

"It's also probably good we're heading up there this morning, as it will give you an idea on how to get up to Daytona Beach tomorrow, which will be just following the same road. I think your decision to miss a day at the show and go see the bikers at the Biketoberfest in Daytona is the best choice and a pretty unique experience. Another world, full of Harleys, and nothing like the classic bikes we saw up in Birmingham. You know the sort—leathers and skimpily-clad bikini girls on the back of the bikes. Lots of people drinking beer and playing around. But it should be fun."

It's true. I'd been curious for some time to bike over to Daytona Beach, on Florida's Atlantic coast, and tomorrow was perfect, due to the fact that there was this massive bike festival going on over the weekend, almost as big as the famous spring Bike Week. Hitting two birds with one stone, I'd also planned to go and visit the historic Daytona Racetrack, which was in close proximity to the beach and everything else that was going on. I guess, also, the thought of a nice fish meal on the beach made it just another reason to bike over, even if it was a two hundred mile round trip.

Another fairly predictable hot, blue sky, Florida morning waits for us outside. I wheel the bike easily out from the garage, now being a lot less heavy and a lot more manoeuvrable without all that luggage on it. Like Mike, I'm also wanting to check the tyres, but with my little tyre gauge I'd bought a few years back in Oklahoma. Before I can, Mike strolls over, curious.

"Don't worry about those. I checked—thirty-eight at the front and forty-one at the back. All done when I did mine."

"That's great. Thanks."

He points into the garage, "That automated pump I have in there is great. It's quick, precise, and I never need go to a gas station, unless I'm on the road." He's so organised.

With both bikes checked, packed for today, and ready to leave, there's nothing more to do than pull our helmets on and head out on this beautiful sunny morning, past the baseball fields and over the railway tracks.

Once again, the morning rush hour is almost non-existent around here as we leave quiet Lake Wales and head north to Orlando.

It's good to be going back on the same route this morning and with places I now recognise. Further up, nearer to Orlando, I'll definitely keep my eyes pinned for any major landmarks, so I'm sure to take the right exit back to Lake Wales later on. Again, I've been told I'll be riding back on my own, so I'll make sure to leave before it gets dark. Riding that far in the dark, and on Interstate 4, would be hell.

The smoothness of Route 27, and the sun on my back makes me smile. The Bonnie is going great. What a bike. "Never a problem," I say, touching my helmeted head for good luck that nothing bad does happen. Mike is also looking happy out front, easily overtaking the few trucks and cars on the road.

Fast forward, and we've hit and turned onto Interstate 4, which is another world. Once again, I'm seeing the traffic quickly building up on this major route, which will lead to the theme parks, Orlando, and over to the east coast to Daytona Beach. After about twenty miles, the familiar signs for Disney, Epcot, and SeaWorld appear and then, just as quickly, I notice we've ridden past the familiar junction leading to the convention center.

I didn't realise how enormous Orlando really is. The highway just seems to go on and on, through massive built-up areas of the city. Until the 1950s, Orlando was not much more than a sleepy country town, but it's proximity to Cape Canaveral and the ever increasing number of theme parks that made it a popular holiday destination for so many Americans helped change all that.

Eleven exits later, I spot a right indicator going on from Mike's bike to get off at Exit 83. I look in my rear view mirror and do the same. He quickly changes lane to the inside, and, before I know it, we're riding along South Grande Avenue that runs parallel to the Interstate.

On this quiet Saturday morning, we ride through a part of downtown Orlando, where glass-sided high-rise buildings on either side of us make it feel like a pretty wealthy business and commercial district. This is actually quite fun. The roads are eerily quiet, with most shops and offices still closed, but it also seems to be the kind of place that will come alive at night, when tourists and locals will flock to the many bars and restaurants, particularly around Orange Avenue, which is Orlando's main street and just one block away from the Ace location.

As Mike said last night, he doesn't normally need to come to this part of Orlando, so it's also a relatively unfamiliar experience for him. I'm not worried. I'm just enjoying riding through this beautiful part of the town.

Just four blocks further up, on our right, we turn onto West Livingston Street, noticing the LYNX Central Station, a bus terminal and connecting rail station for the SunRail commuter train in Orlando. From there, it's then easy walking distance to Orlando's businesses, shopping, entertainment, and nightclubs.

We've arrived at our destination and on the opposite side from the station is the H2O building, soon to be Ace Cafe USA on 100 West Livingston Street.

We ride into a large, empty car park, with just a few vehicles and bikes already there. We stop in front of a red-bricked building which is almost industrial in looks, with a large sign saying "H2O Church" over the facade of the main entrance. At the same time, a beautiful, yellow convertible Corvette arrives—a throwback from the '60s, with its beautiful chrome bumpers and lush leather seats. An equally sophisticated and sun-glassed lady with scarf wrapped around her head neatly parks it next to the Bonnevilles and then wanders casually into the building.

Pulling off my helmet, I see a friendly face approaching. It's Linda, wife of Mark Wilsmore, the founder of The Ace Cafe in London.

"Good morning, Zoë. You've obviously found the place! We still haven't got any signs up for it here yet, as the building and construction work hasn't even started."

I walk towards her. "Hey. Linda. Good to see you. Have you met Mike?"

They both shake hands, with Linda continuing, "Let's go take a walk and look in the gardens around the building and out at the back. They say there's quite a bit of history here. Then we can go inside for a coffee and hear from the guys what's being planned."

We wander out into the warm morning sunshine and around into a grassy, palm tree lined area, which doesn't seem to have been used for quite a while. Towards the back is fencing, with what looks like a rail track behind it. It's amazing that a tropical, hidden place like this still exists in such a prime downtown location. At this moment in time, it's difficult to imagine what this massive place will look like once it's all finished.

In front of us is an old, dilapidated wood panelled outbuilding, which we walk up to and peer inside. Mike opens his mouth and eyes with astonishment. "Oh, boy, this is pretty amazing! Look up at the ceiling. That's an overhead steam-driven belt system. This place must have been one of the repair stations for the steam locomotives here. This is fantastic. This must be why the place is right next to the tracks."

We look behind us and through the fence and, as he said, there are, indeed, rail tracks. This place must definitely have a story and a half to tell.

I nod, "Wow! A bit of history. I wonder if it'll be kept?"

By the time we've walked back, all sorts of interesting cars and bikes, and mostly cafe racers, have arrived. We go into the building which is now a skeleton of its former self. Someone said it had been a famous nightclub. The place, although empty, is spectacular, with what looks like a massive dance floor and stage. I look up and see there are three levels, with a large, deep wraparound balcony overlooking the stage and pit areas. This must have been quite a place, and I want to know more!

We walk around the balcony and grab a coffee and bagel. Everyone else, now probably about sixty people, are curiously looking into the rooms and areas within the building. Mike and I pour another coffee and start chatting to a local guy, who can't be more informative about what this place is all about.

"Well, you're really in a piece of Orlando history from the music scene, which has seen a lot of things and about which, I'm sure, the guys are gonna talk about. But it's currently, believe it or not, home to the H2O Church, a highly progressive and faith-based organisation. Only up until recently, they also managed it as a music venue called H2O Live for national and world tours. It's the location—so easy to get to."

I'd never have believed it was a church, but it seems like this place has had a number of different reincarnations.

And, with that, Mark Wilsmore casually walks up onto the stage with the rest of his crew.

"Morning guys. Thanks for coming today to see the place before the work on it gets started. I also wanted to take this opportunity to talk a bit about our own history at The Ace, and why we're so excited about it coming to the US."

Everyone nods in appreciation. This is going to be interesting. I didn't really know a lot about the history of the London Ace Cafe, and what we're about to hear and learn is truly inspiring.

The Ace Cafe is a true icon of British culture and history. The Cafe's motoring heritage dates back to November 1938, just before World War Two, when it was built as a roadside cafe to cater for the truckers and motorists using the newly-built North Circular Road around London. Once established, the owner, Hugo Edenborough, better known as Vic Edenborough, turned his thoughts to the motor trade, and, in August 1939, he opened a service station with a battery of ten pumps on adjoining land, with a spacious washing bay, showroom and repair shops.

But only a fortnight later, World War Two was declared, petrol rationing in England was immediately introduced, and, with no other choice, most vehicles were no longer used or were simply locked away in garages. Things looked bleak, and, horrendously, in November 1940, the cafe received a direct hit from a bomb and was completely destroyed. A temporary building was quickly erected, so that business, although on a limited scale, could continue to service the community.

With a strong patriotic desire to contribute in some way, Vic Edenborough amazingly soon turned his attention to serious war work. By 1943 new buildings had been erected, with machine tools installed. A hundred and twenty people were employed as direct contractors to the M.A.P. (Ministry of Aircraft Production), specialising in the production of steel components for aircraft. Just a year later, in 1944, the Ace Service Station was operating engineering shops reputed to be the finest of their scale in the country. Continuing during the war period, the petrol station was kept open, being one of the very few that, amazingly, gave an all-night service.

After the war, the production facility was no longer needed and quickly closed. Once again, the dynamic and visionary founder, Mr. Edenborough, had the showrooms redesigned. He made proposals to leading British car manufacturers, which led him to becoming a stockist for Austin, Standard, Triumph, Daimler, and Lanchester, which in turn, led him to also being appointed distributor for the French Citroën cars. The showroom accommodated twenty-five vehicles and was believed to be at the time the biggest in London. It also had a team of first class mechanics, capable of handling any job from engine tuning to complete overhauls.

One employee, John Wyer, went on to manage the Aston Martin, Gulf Ford GT40, and Porsche 917 sports car racing campaigns. Racing celebrities seemed to pour through the doors. The racing driver, Earl Howe, was a regular at the Ace, along with many motoring journalists and photographers. It's said that even Sir Malcolm Campbell spent the night at The Ace, albeit sadly in a hearse on the way to his own funeral. This English racing motorist had gained the world speed record on land and on water during the 1920s and 1930s using famous vehicles called the Blue Bird. He was one of the few land speed record holders of his era to die of natural causes, as so many died in crashes in those dangerous times.

By 1949, the Cafe had been completely rebuilt and was then a new state-of-the-art cafe and one of the first places to use neon signage to attract the customers. With its proximity to Britain's new and fast network of roads, and, incredibly, staying open twenty-four hours, unsurprisingly the cafe was soon attracting hoards of young motorcyclists who were bored and looking for their own identity. They soon found it at the Ace Cafe.

The rise of the teenager in the early fifties saw the Ace booming, with the arrival of the Ton-Up Boys. These were the kids who could reach the magic number of 100 mph on their bikes.

The British motorcycle industry, with the likes of Triumph, BSA, Royal Enfield, Ariel, and Norton was at its peak, when along came rock 'n' roll, or the "devil's music," from the USA! It wasn't played on radio stations, so the only places it could be heard were at travelling fairgrounds or on jukeboxes in transport cafes.

With this powerful and toxic new mixture of motorbikes and rock 'n' roll, came the stories of "record racing." The Ton-Up boys would drop a coin into the slot of the jukebox, run to their bikes, then race to a given point and try and get back again before the record finished. This ultimately turned the likes of the Ace Cafe on the North Circular Road, the Ace of Spades in South London, and the Chelsea Bridge tea stall as "unofficial race track" destinations.

With the sixties, the Rocker had emerged, and the Ace Cafe became the launching venue for many British rock 'n' roll bands, like Johnny Kidd & The Pirates. Gene Vincent also visited the Cafe on one of his tours, and there's word that The Beatles had been there before they became famous.

But, just as quickly as it had appeared, the early rock 'n' roll mania was over by the mid-sixties, pushed to one side with the likes of The Beatles, the fashion of London's Carnaby Street, and the rise of the Mod era. With people now earning more money and able to afford cars, this came at the expense of the motorbike, and, with the retirement of the owner, the Ace Cafe, now viewed only as a "greasy spoon," served its last egg and chips in 1969.

In the following years, the building was used for many different things. from a filling station, bookmakers, vehicle distributors, and tyre depot, but, fortunately, it remained largely unaltered.

Then, in 1993, Mark Wilsmore, driven by his passion for bikes, rock 'n' roll, and history, and with the permission of the current owners, set about planning an event to mark the twenty-fifth anniversary of the Cafe's closure. He had in mind to re-open the place. Incredibly, in September 1994, the event attracted an amazing 12,000 motorcyclists and rock 'n' roll fans!

The grand re-opening of The Ace was in September, 2001. Today, The Ace is a fully licensed cafe-restaurant, events, and music venue, with its own shop and plenty of reminders on the walls about its colourful history when it was first home to the Ton-Up-Boys (and girls) and Rockers. With its rich heritage and traditions, diverse and eclectic meets are held throughout the year to cater for all car and bike enthusiasts. Without a doubt, it's still the key hangout in London for rockers, bikers, and petrol heads, alike. And you can even get married there!

That reminds me. There's been many an occasion that I've been there and experienced those amazing bike days, including trips with everyone down to the South Coast on sunny bank holiday weekends. The inspiration for my first trip across America was even made there!

Everyone claps with enthusiasm and admiration, and the microphone is quickly passed to Steve, from Ace USA. "Thanks again for you guys making it down here this morning. We're looking to start working on the site next year, with the planning permission now sorted. I know that we have some press here today and, of course, all our friends who've helped us along the way, but we thought you'd be interested to know that we seriously considered where the best place for the Ace USA should be. We'd even looked as far away as Los Angeles, but this place just makes so much sense.

"I'm glad you've had a chance to look around. We wanted a place with soul and a history that we could follow. This place certainly has it! The H2O Live, as it's known here at the moment, has an awesome and legendary history back to the '90s, when it was Central Florida's largest rock venue, called The Edge Pavilion.

"The Edge opened from early 1992 to the summer of 1996 and started life as an alternative rock club, hosting early career gigs by the likes of Pearl Jam, Nine Inch Nails, Blur, and many others. Thanks to the efforts of DJ Icey, these awesome rock shows were complemented by after-hours dance nights, which would often kick-off around midnight and go until the very early morning. Due to its large capacity, The Edge also hosted enormous raves on holiday weekends that would draw thousands. This was just one of the venues, like AAHZ and Simon's, that propelled Orlando's Electric Dance Music culture in the '90s and cemented Orlando's party credentials.

"Incredibly, and something totally different, in 2000 the place was taken over and became a well-known Country and Western Club called '8 Seconds', with crazy bull riding inside and out. It's been a mega venue that over the years has hosted many international acts like Nirvana, Ted Nugent, Lenny Kravitz, and the list goes on. So, you could say, it's just a big, legendary downtown rock house with some serious mojo! So, there you go, that's why we gotta have The Ace here—more living history!"

Afterwards, still munching on muffins and bagels and drinking hot coffee, we're all shown pictures and artists' impressions of what the Ace Cafe USA will look like in just under a year. The vision will be showrooms for all sorts of bikes, gift shops, a great place to eat, and, of course, music and vehicle events running on a packed agenda like the Ace in London. The place is amazing, and I can already imagine what it will become—bikes, cars, rock 'n' roll, not to mention speed, thrills, and just a bit of rebellion.

Before too long, I can see Mike looking discreetly down to his watch, and I nod in understanding. We walk back out into the sunshine, but, before putting my helmet on, I walk over to the sexy Corvette and see the sun-glassed woman chatting to a cool looking dude next to it. I can't resist asking. She nods, smiling, and hands me the keys. I unlock the chrome handle on the door and slide down into the soft, old leather seat, dreaming I'm driving down a palm lined beach somewhere in the Keys—one day, maybe!

Walking over to the bike while putting my helmet on, I see Mike is already on his bike and starting up. No rush, please. Got to get myself sorted. I climb onto the bike, start it up, and we sweep out of the large driveway and head south, back onto the mayhem of Interstate 4 to the Orange County Convention Center.

AIMExpo is in full swing when we arrive, obvious now because it's now almost impossible to find space for our bikes in the massive field-sized parking lot. We seem to ride round and round for a while, until I see Mike enthusiastically pointing to a space right in the middle. How I'm going to find my bike later on is anyone's guess.

The smiling faces of Rich and Gary, from RokStraps, greet me as I walk up to them to spend a few hours with them signing the books.

"You guys should have gone over to the Ace this morning. Quite a place and quite a project!"

And, with that, between chatting with people telling their own adventures, I recount the stories about The Ace to Rich and Gary, who seem mesmerized with it all.

Before too long, it's another day which has just disappeared and the last day at the show for me. It was quite an experience and one I won't forget for a long time. But the thought of getting back out onto the road tomorrow and heading for the beach seems a lot more tempting in my eyes.

Mike, still sitting behind the counter of the Vintage Japanese Motorcycle Club, hands me my helmet. "Now, Zoë, how do you feel about getting back tonight on your own again. You think you'll be alright?"

"Yes, I'm getting pretty familiar with the route now. It's the traffic getting out of here, though, which is hell."

"Yea. Take it easy and be careful. Some guys who came over here said they'd seen an accident southbound, so you may be delayed. But don't forget you can't filter."

I smile, knowing he knows I'm impatient.

No more than a couple of miles from the exhibition center, and before hitting the theme parks, the traffic has come to a total standstill, and I'm sitting on my bike with my feet on the ground balancing it—waiting, and waiting, and waiting. The traffic is not moving. It's hot, and I have no shade.

I can start to feel the sweat coming from under my helmet, down my face, and down my neck. I open my tank bag, pull out a flannel cloth, and, pulling up my visor, wipe my face. Damn, I also thought I'd put a bottle of water in there, too. I'm thirsty. It must be in the side bags, which I can't get to. Most cars have now even turned off their engines.

I lean to one side to look through the traffic into the hazy distance with the sun in my eyes and seem to see tiny red lights flashing. That must be where the accident is. I can wait, but I'm not sure I can wait that long with the heat pounding down on me. Please hurry. Even the driver in his air-conditioned car next to me is looking at me with a little bit of sympathy.

Suddenly, loud sounds come from behind, and the traffic behind and next to me is quickly moving to each side to let two ambulances speed through. Now, if that was the UK, I'd have quickly started up and followed them through the traffic, but, here, it somehow feels not quite right. So I watch them go through, hoping we'll all be able to move off again very, very soon.

I'm sweating. I'm boiling. There's no respite from the sun hitting down on me and onto my face. I seem to be sitting on that bike, waiting forever. I close my eyes, trying to think of something cool like a nice fresh swimming pool or an iced beer bottle sliding down my face and arms. And the sun's making me dozy.

Suddenly, I'm jolted back to reality. Miraculously, just as quickly as it had stopped, the traffic starts to move, and soon I can feel the warm breeze flowing past me once again, which seems like a gift from heaven.

I thankfully remember the landmarks we'd again passed this morning and, feeling a lot more confident with the route, successfully exit back down onto Route 27 South to Lake Wales. The sun is now quickly starting to go down over the fields. I accelerate slightly, and it's not long before I see the familiar McDonalds and quickly turn left and over the bumpy railway tracks.

Mike's kids, Tess and Jacob, are in the garden when I arrive, playing with their miniature Mexican Chihuahua. I stop and pull up my visor to say hello. They reel back in horror, then start giggling. What's going on?

I pull the keys out. "Hi, guys. What is it?"

Tess looks at her brother as if to say, "Should we tell her?" then says, "Have you been to the beach? Half your face is red and the other half is white!"

I lean down and look in the bike's side mirror. I gasp. She's right. I look awful. From my nose down to my neck I'm red. It must have been when I was waiting in the accident traffic with the sun blaring down on me and the visor down, but I hadn't realized it was that strong.

I nod, smiling to go along with the joke, "Yes, I was sunbathing with my helmet on! I couldn't get it off!"

They giggle even more and run off chasing the hairless Chihuahua, no doubt wanting to put suntan cream on it!

15

RACE TO DAYTONA

Lake Wales, Florida to Daytona Beach, Florida and back

228 miles

I lean over and squint into the bathroom mirror. I'm reassured that my red face, from my neck up to my nose, has mellowed over night, and that I don't look like some freak party animal heading up to Daytona.

There's a loud, impatient knock on the bathroom door. It's Jacob. "Are you done yet? Dad wants to get to the show. I'm gonna go with him on the bike and need to find my socks quick!"

"Just give me two. I'm almost done."

Walking out, with Jacob running in, I hear another anxious shout down the corridor. This time it's Mike. "Hey, guys. We gotta get a move on today. We'll grab a bite to eat on the way over."

I follow where the voice is coming from and walk into the kitchen, where Mike is dressed in his biking gear, looking like he's ready to go and already pulling his boots on.

"Morning, Mike. Tell me the truth. How do I look? Has the sunburn gone down? I can't believe I was stuck standing on that highway last night for almost half an hour."

He pretends to retain a laugh and with pursed lips says, "Let's put it this way. You look better than last night. I thought you'd been on a BBQ grill on the way back!"

"Oh stop. You know how sensitive I am."

"You look fine. You just look like you've been out on the road."

I don't really know how to take that comment but interpret it as healthy and glowing.

Within ten minutes, all three of us have walked out to the garage and pushed the two bikes out. It's another lovely day, without any luggage on the bike.

Handing me a piece of paper Mike peers over it with me. "Remember what we talked about last night. Well, here's a rough map I drew up to show you more easily where you need to get to. When we turn off for the show, you just continue going straight up the same Interstate 4, off onto Interstate 95 North for a bit, then immediately east onto the International Speedway Boulevard, where you'll go right past the Daytona International Speedway. You're gonna, no doubt, start seeing bikes speeding down that highway."

Running his finger along the route, he continues, "Through the town and over the bridge onto Atlantic Avenue, which is real nice, running along the beach. I've also put on the map two crazy places you may want to check out to see what Biketoberfest is all about—the Iron Horse Saloon and the Cabbage Patch. The first one is a bit further up along the beach. You can cross back over by Ormond Beach and go see this fun place on US Route 1 that only opens for the bike rallies. I wish I was going just for that!"

It sounds like he has some interesting memories of it. "Yea, the Iron Horse Saloon is just north of the Tomoka River. It has an overhead walkway where you can look down onto the stage with the music and action going on. There's a lot of bars up there, too. People ride right into the bar and park their bikes below the walkway. They get big name bands there during Bike Week and are famous for their beef tips. If you have time, try to also get to the Cabbage Patch, another famous place for the bikers, but further south and inland from the beach."

I'm intrigued and continue listening while Mike enthusiastically explains, "This other place. You gotta see it. It's famous for their "Cabbage Wrestling!" They have a big ring and fill it with coleslaw. Then girls in bikinis get in a wrestling match together. It's quite a show for them and the spectators. They've also got a bunch of good bands playing during Bike Week and Biketoberfest. There's also lots of food and bike accessory and clothing vendors there. You know the stuff—mostly "pirate" garb, leather everything. You'll never believe it when you see it, but the rest of the year the place is a tiny little bar on the corner, not much bigger than Fuzzy's, the local bar we went to the other night here in Lake Wales."

Jacob's eyes open wide in astonishment, like he can't quite believe what he's just heard his Dad talk about.

"Then you come back the same way along the beach or, if you want, but not so picturesque, hop onto I-95 again, which will lead you back onto I-4. Got it?"

Wow, it's quite a bit to absorb, and it seems like a massive amount to see and experience in just a few hours. I look intently down at the pencil drawn map, scratching my head.

He can see I'm looking at it questioningly and adds, reassuring me, "If nothing else, try and get down to the pier and then bike or walk along Main Street where the action is. You know the sort—bars, souvenir shops, tattoo parlors, leather clad guys with their bikini wearing half-clad chicks on their Harleys and choppers, cruising down Main Street for everyone to see them. It's quite a sight."

I carefully flatten out this new map and put it into the top of my clear tank bag pocket, which I'll quickly peer down at when I'm needing directions. It's good to be just a bit organized. Instinctively today, I've got a better than normal feeling, riding half the way with Mike and Jacob, that the rest is going to be pretty straight forward. It should be a good Sunday morning run. I'm also hoping to see a lot more bikes out on the roads heading up the same way to Daytona.

Now, almost now like a daily ritual, I watch Mike start up, and I do the same. Both bikes purr contentedly. Jacob climbs onto the back of Mike's bike and holds him around the waist, with his feet just touching the foot rests, he looks round and smiles to me. I grin and smile back.

Then it's off, without further ado, along the quiet lake lined roads, over the lumpy railway tracks, and out onto the country highway.

I'm feeling good, without a worry, and breathe in the warm air, knowing I've got to make the most of it, as this will be the last day on the road before returning the bike back to the guys at Lakeland. But I don't want to think about that too much now. I just want to enjoy the day and see and experience new things, which is what I love when you're the master of your own time.

Florida has really been an eye-opener to me in so many ways, from seeing lost and remote farming towns with their own cowboys and following the beautiful Gulf of Mexico coastline with its heavenly wild beaches and in contrast to the glamorous sophisticated resorts close to Sarasota.

Just before we hit the busy junction with I-4 into Orlando, I see Mike looking around. He's obviously looking for the right exit and wanting to get somewhere. I reckon it's for our much needed breakfast. And there we go! Keeping a close eye on him, I see him signal and swerve into the inside lane, and he's getting off at the next exit, with me quickly following. We continue down a smaller road and, almost immediately, at the junction see our beloved McDonalds.

Soon we're all sitting at a table eating Egg McMuffins, bacon, and pretty much anything else that goes with it and onto the plate. I'm not proud.

Mike finishes a big mouthful of hash browns. "So remember. We're not going to stop. I'll just signal when we're leaving the highway, and you'll just continue up the same road. Some of it should look familiar because we went further up on it just yesterday to see The Ace. Then make your way back anytime. We'll also try and not be back too late, as it's your last night here with us."

I nod in total agreement. "Exactly. We should all go out for some drinks and a bite to eat. It's on me. It's the least I can do. This has just been the most incredible trip. You've shown me places I wouldn't have even imagined existed."

He smiles. "As I said, there's even more over at Daytona that you'll never have seen before!"

I don't doubt that for one moment but I'm also imagining it's going to be one mega commercial place for tourists and the bikers coming into town over the next few days. It's a place, I know, that drink and scantily clad chicks play a major role. The place wouldn't exactly be my first choice to spend a lot of time at, but to go there for a one day experience and hopefully get an eyeful of it all, plus the famous racetrack, will be just fine with me. It's going to be fun, or at least very different from what I've seen here so far.

It's not long before we approach, once again and the last time for me, the convention center exit. With a smile, I see Mike pointing his finger fervently straight ahead, which I guess is him saying where I need to go. I honk the horn, which is actually quite a weak noise, and Mike honks back, which is much louder.

With Jacob waving me goodbye, they quickly disappear, and, for the last time, I'm on the road all on my own again, riding to another place I've never been to. It feels good. Now I can go at any speed I want, I can slow down when I want, I can speed up when I want, I can stop and get gas when I want. In fact I can do anything. Well, almost. The day's all mine.

I look up to the sun, which is directly overhead, not having forgotten to put lots of cream on my face and leaving downtown Orlando immediately see signs that I'm just fifty-five miles away from Daytona and the Atlantic Coast. So, all in all, if all goes well, it shouldn't take me much more than an hour before I see the sea.

It has to be said that Interstate 4 from Orlando to Daytona is nothing that mind blowing. Fine, it's a lot quieter on this side than the mayhem on Disney's side, but, besides a lot of arid looking farmland and small towns I go past like Deltona and Lake Helen, there's nothing really much to write home about or stop off for.

But there is one major thing I'm noticing, and that's bikes. I've been amazed riding through this part of America how few of them we've actually seen or encountered on our journeys back and forth along the roads through Florida. But today is different. Bikes of all sorts, from racers to choppers, are entering the highway and making their way north to the coast and Daytona.

I look down at Mike's crumpled map on my tank and double check if it actually is 95 North I need to get on. Best to double check numbers. This is, in fact, the main highway that hugs the entire east coast of Florida for more than three hundred and forty-five miles from Jacksonville to Miami. More importantly, it's also one of the major routes in the US, running almost 2,000 miles down the entire East Coast, from way up north in Maine in New England to sunny Miami at the tip of Florida.

It looks like I'm only on it for a few miles before jumping eastwards onto US Route 92, better known to everyone around here as the famous International Speedway Boulevard, and home to the Holy Grail of raceways, the Daytona International Speedway. This dual carriageway is already feeling like it's close to the sea, with palm trees lining the roads. More and more bikes are now appearing and stopping alongside me at the numerous sets of traffic lights before impatiently thundering off to the beach.

So, what am I going to do? Am I also going directly to the beach or maybe making a stop at the Speedway? I'm already seeing signs for it and then, before I know it, I'm indicating into its parking area and stop alongside a large red metallic touring Harley.

I'll take a little wander. I walk through the large glass fronted building opening into a large atrium. It's definitely not a race day, or this place would be heaving. It already feels like a place for racing. I look up, and around the wall are arches, with photographs around them showing the history of the place, and above them are orange and green race lights, indicating "stop and go."

Daytona's very own "World Center of Racing" attracts thousands of race fans every year, and people from around the world attend the eight major racing weekends held annually at the track, which holds about 160,000 spectators.

Probably more important as a title is its being the "Birthplace of NASCAR," which began here in 1947. It's hard to believe, but it dates even further back to 1902 to the drag races held on Daytona's long hard sand beaches. So, as I read on the panels on the walls, NASCAR (National Association for Stock Car Auto Racing) is the main pull here throughout the year. There's definitely no racing going on today, but I am curious to somehow see the racetrack. Maybe I'll have the opportunity to wander the massive stands for free or take a "first-come-first-served" half hour tram tour around the speedway track and pit area. But these tours I've sadly missed.

Not giving up, I wander past the gift shop and outside, seeing the curved stands from the distance. A guard approaches me, trying to wave me away. "Morning, Ma'am. The racetrack is currently closed. You won't see much here."

He's right. The tall Speedway walls and view out onto the track are covered, so there's no chance to peep through. I can wait two hours for the next tour or head out. I think I'll take the second option, as time is running away from me, and, anyway, it would have been better to experience this place on an actual race day.

I walk back out, and the Harley's disappeared. I turn right, or eastwards, to the sea and continue into downtown Daytona, where I start seeing shops selling the usual paraphernalia of beach necessities like floating blow-up chairs, surf boards, beach chairs, towels, T-shirts, kayaks, and kites. It still very much looks like a built-up town you'd see pretty much anywhere stretching along the anonymous highway.

It's not until I reach the last intersection with Interstate 95 that, just two blocks farther on, I cross a massive bridge over the Halifax River and onto the strip of Daytona Beach, with the Atlantic on the other side.

The instructions from Mike were to ride up along the beach road, or Atlantic Avenue, which I'm now on. I slowly "cruise," as they say, with other bikers along this long, straight road with its tall apartment and hotel blocks on the sea side. Lower buildings with, what look like, masses of restaurant chains and bars stuffed with people and bikes are on the other side of the road. And, yes, there are a lot of bikers doing the same as me, just absorbing it all out on the road. Maybe not as many as I'd expected but still a lot, and quite a few going well over the speed limits. And any Bonnevilles? Well, not really, only mine!

I continue along the coastal road, using Mike's directions, and head back onto the mainland to go visit the first joint he avidly recommended. I join a quiet forest lined road and then see something I just can't miss, which is on the other side of the road. A massive sign, at least fifty feet high: "World Famous Iron Horse Saloon." Lines of shining, gleaming bikes are being marshalled to quickly park outside the entrance on the edge of the road. There must already be too many bikes inside and it's full. There are bronzed, jean and leather-clad people walking around looking at the bikes and entering the grounds. It looks, from what I can see, like a big show inside, with lots of tents selling clothes, sunglasses, and normal event bric-a-brac. Payment is needed to enter this place, which surprises me. I'm not convinced. I can't drink, so I can't really make the most of the place and the party festivities.

One of the marshals approaches, seeing I've parked the bike up away from the others. "You can't just park your bike on the road. You'll need to go over there and park between those other bikes."

"It's OK. I'm coming here just to see what it's about."

"Good, no problem. But you'll need to move pretty soon as bikes are coming in fast now."

That's fine by me. I soak in the atmosphere of everybody coming and going for a while longer, then get back on the bike and head to Mike's biggest recommendation, the Cabbage Patch with the girl coleslaw wrestlers! I look down at the map and see it's quite a few miles out of town, back south off I-95. I think I'll give it a miss, although I would have loved to hear the referee say to the girls, "I need slaw on both shoulders for you to win!"

I have to say, looking at both options, the idea of seeing Daytona Beach, the Atlantic Ocean and its waves, absorbing the atmosphere on Main Street with all the bikers going down it, walking the boardwalk pier, and maybe along the beach with a bit of sand in between my toes, plus possibly finding a nice place for lunch far outweigh the coleslaw wrestling.

So I head back along the coast to Atlantic Avenue. Riding through town, I can see why stretches of Daytona Beach were once the city's incredible raceway. These wide, hard-packed and white sandy beaches just seem to go on and on into the horizon. Apparently, some sections of the beach still welcome drivers to the sands farther up, but this time at a strictly enforced low speed limit.

I then spot signs for Main Street Pier and Boardwalk, which, amazingly and very conveniently, are simply at the end of Main Street. Perfect. I ride to the top of it, which overlooks the beach and sea. I've lucked out. I park the bike tightly between two other bikes, which is one of the last remaining spots on the street. I change my boots to flip-flops, chain my helmet onto the bike, and put on my baseball hat. I'm ready to take a stroll.

The place feels frantic. Tourists are walking, some drinking beers in brown paper bags, along the sidewalk and heading down to where the biking action is going on farther down Main Street. But I don't quite want that yet. I want to go down to the famous miles and miles of beach, where the racing started to make this place so famous. I walk to the top of the road and out in front see the beach.

With typical Floridian hype, Daytona Beach bills itself as "The World's Most Famous Beach." But its fame is less about quality than the size of the parties this expansive beach has witnessed, particularly during Spring Break. Then there are, of course, the Speed Weeks and the motorcycle events, when it's said that half a million bikers roar into town for the main Bike Week in March and then thousands this weekend for Biketoberfest.

I walk along the sandy, palm lined boardwalk, where an enormous ferris wheel dominates the skyline. I'm a little taken back by the place, as it seems a little "worn around the edges"—nothing like Longboat Key. Here there are lots of gaudy carnival attractions, dollar grabbing ice-cream shops, amusement arcades, and people sipping beer on the patios from plastic cups. I don't know if I'd call it sleazy, but it's a little reminiscent of Blackpool back at home, where the drinking and nightlife is very prominent. The beach is, indeed, incredibly long, without an end in sight and rows of not so stylish hotels and oldish, say '60s or '70s looking tall apartment blocks lining it as far as the eye can see.

This place was a lot different and a lot more stylish a long time ago. In 1902, Ransom Olds, a guest staying at the Ormond Hotel, noticed just how easy it was to drive his racing car, the "Pirate," on the hard, sandy beach, and, what better he thought than to race on it. So the following year, in 1903, Ransom Olds, of Oldsmobile fame, challenged Scottish born Alexander Winton, automobile designer and founder of the Winton Motor Carriage Company, and Oscar Hedstrom, the only one on a motorcycle and co-founder of the Indian Motorcycle Manufacturing company and Indian Motorcycle, to a high-profile race along the unusually hard-packed sandy shore. The race reached an unheard of top speed of fifty-seven miles per hour. Winton won in his car—Bullet No 1.

These were the first exciting speed trials, which continued over the next thirty years, where speed records were set and shattered. During the Prohibition Period, production of moonshine—the illegal corn liquor with a kick like a lightening bolt—was an essential part of the Southern economy, and renegades with cars speedy enough to outrun the police handled the illegal distribution. With a knack of fast driving, during their time off, they raced each other. When Prohibition was abolished, the races continued.

Stock car racing came into vogue during the late 1930s, and the "Race Weeks" literally packed the beaches with fans. The most seductive venue was Daytona's Beach Street track, where the driver, Bill France, started promoting these Race Weeks. The sport exploded, but with some dismissing it as only rednecks racing cars any mechanic could build. Maybe not quite! Amazingly, The "Bluebird Streamliner" was driven to a new world record for the measured mile by Malcolm Campbell at Ormond Beach in 1935! Powered by a Rolls-Royce engine, the car reached incredible speeds of just over 276 mph.

Mister France knew what he was on to and, in 1947, set about transforming his obsession into a world class sporting competition. NASCAR was created and is now regarded as the most-watched sport in America after football. But, in 1953, Bill France, who had entered the inaugural historic stock car race, saw that the fast growth of Daytona Beach and its holiday attractions would soon put an end to these beach races. It was at that time that he proposed the construction of the current Daytona International Speedway. It's hard to believe that it wasn't until 1959 that the racing was finally relocated from the beach to the Speedway, now one of the world's most important race tracks, and where the cars are still everyday autos conforming to strict regulations, and it's the driver and pit crew—not the car—that are tested!

Fortunately, its famous twenty-three mile beach is still one of the few in Florida where cars are still allowed on the sands, a true hangover from the days more than a hundred years ago when the first enthusiasts raced along them. I hope it continues.

I turn back, wanting to feel the famous sand for myself. I take my flip-flops off, go down the steps, and walk out onto the sandy beach and approach the unmissable Main Street Pier. All my perceptions of a cheap, well-worn place change. Here, I see beauty. I walk underneath it, through its tall, wooden, supporting stilted legs with a few seagulls flying through it and enjoy the short respite of shade. Built in 1930 and re-opened after restoration in 2012, this eighty-five year old beautiful Art Deco white and turquoise looking wooden structure is incredible, jutting out two hundred and thirty-seven metres out into the wild Atlantic Ocean, making it the longest pier in the United States.

I walk back up the stairs and walk out along the pier. Smack in the middle of this majestic pier is my dream come true—Joe's Crab Shack, with views looking out onto the blue sea. I grab one of the last remaining outdoor tables on the wooden boards and contentedly sit, looking down at the people walking along the beach and the surfers and guys windsailing out at sea. The choice is an easy one. Joe's Classic Steampot of succulent shrimp and queen crab is ordered, and I'm shortly pulling the crab claws clean and luxuriating in seventh heaven.

This could be a world away from what I've just seen out at the Iron Horse Saloon and what I'm expecting to encounter back down on Main Street, with more and more bikers arriving and with the voyeurism of people coming to inquisitively experience the proceedings, but at this moment, I'm just going to absorb this wonderful part of Daytona's old heritage while listening to the waves crashing up under the pier and tucking into the delicious, fresh seafood.

Time is running away from me, so, after taking my bib off and washing my hands clean, I wander back down to Main Street, wanting to check that the bike is OK. You never know, when there are so many people wandering around and bikes parking so close up, but it seems to be just fine. Even a few people are curiously looking at it, which I always like and which makes me smile. I cross over the busy, congested junction full of cars and bikes and over to the "party" side of Main Street. It's been closed off for all traffic except for the bikes now riding down it and maybe trying to find a place to park.

It's crazy. The pavements are so crammed with people that I'm obliged to walk out onto the street, which isn't the best or safest option, with the hundreds of bikes riding so closely past me.

I think there's a lot of people on Main Street. This isn't even the big event, which is Bike Week in March, when, for ten days, it's said that half a million bikers drool over each other's hogs and party round the clock. More drinking, bikes, burly blokes, and busty babes. And during Spring Break as many as 200,000 exuberant, hormone-fuelled youths from all over the US come into town and onto the beach to party.

And the shops! Well, they're the epitome of raucous party goers: T-shirts with every shocking word and expletive on them, shorts that look like they wouldn't even cover your backside, leather jackets and clothing, and tattoo parlours, and between every shop is a bar, and then more bars, with music of all descriptions blaring and belting out from them. In fact, I reckon not to be out of place, you've got to shop with a beer in your hand.

I go to cross the busy road, waiting for a few bikes to pass, when a massive and bizarre vehicle approaches. I can only describe it as a car that the Flintstones would have driven. It looks like it's been made out of wood, and the two guys in it are dressed like prehistoric celebrities with leather, ripped garments and waving to the admiring spectators. Only here!

The throngs of people are getting bigger, if that's possible, and the traffic in the street has almost come to a standstill with the ever increasing number of bikes coming down it.

Before long, it's almost impossible to walk in a straight line for more than a couple of yards.

I've got a feeling that I've "done" Daytona for today, and what I'd really like to do is just jump on my bike and ride back and spend the time I have left in the quieter parts of Florida towards Lake Wales.

But, before all that, I've got to get myself psyched up to navigating out of Daytona and getting through Orlando, which, hopefully, now being mid afternoon on a Sunday, won't be that bad. Well, it would be anywhere else. I've still got to go past Disney, and on a Sunday there's bound to be loads of people coming and going to the theme parks. So I'm not going to speak too soon, as that would ruin everything. The last thing I want is to encounter another accident and another red face.

So I say goodbye to sunny Daytona Beach, which has shown me, even in this short time, a complete diversity of things. It's maybe not a place I'd automatically volunteer to come back to, but the energy is incredible, and, if there was an invitation to come and see the racing, then just maybe I'd nod my head and put my hand up.

The ride back is great. I'm appreciating every single moment of just being one entity with the bike. I recently read something, which I'd found pretty thought provoking. It said that the only way you can really experience the sensation of flying is when you're on a bike. Nothing on or around you, and only the energy underneath you making you fly through the air with the wind going past you—a nice thought.

Thankfully, and maybe because of a bit of experience under my belt now, I get out at the right exit back southwards onto Route 27 and, finally, to Lake Wales, not forgetting to stand up over the railway tracks, stop at the junction if there's no traffic coming, and indicate to absolutely no one.

By the time I reach the house, the sun's starting to go down, and, just as I'm wheeling the bike into the garage, I incredibly hear the other Bonneville also ride up into the driveway.

Mike and Jacob come to a halt on the grass, and the engine's turned off. "Hi, Zoë. So how was it? We stopped at the supermarket to get some drinks and chips on the way back. Otherwise we probably would have got here ahead of you. The show was good but was starting to get quiet later in the afternoon with everyone packing up."

Jacob jumps off and runs inside, no doubt looking for the Chihuahua, while Mike pushes his bike inside, taking his helmet off and placing it on the shelf. "So, how were the boys up in Daytona? We thought it would be good to get back and have a drink on the terrace before heading out for dinner later on, as it's your last day with us. It's been a fun couple of weeks! Even I saw stuff I hadn't seen before!"

Just a short while later, all five of us are sitting happily outside under the clear starry sky, exchanging our stories of the day. Mike was obviously disappointed that I hadn't seen the coleslaw wrestling but it was probably not a bad thing if I'd then had to explain what went on in front of the kids.

For the first time, here in lovely Lake Wales, we all squeeze into the family car, with Andrea driving, and head to one of their favourite locals, "Mannys Original Chop House." For the next couple of hours, between eating great steak, the kids running back and forth, and some of us drinking beers, we talk animatedly about everything we'd done and seen out on the road over the past few weeks.

This has been one hell of a road trip and so very unique. This time we really did take the lesser known routes, and how good was that?! The places were so eclectic, places that I would never have normally even envisaged going to or even known existed. That's the beauty of it. I guess you could call it a road trip of unexpected and unplanned surprises, which I'm so glad I trusted my Road Dog travelling companion to plan and bring to life. Florida, Alabama, and Georgia have been eye-openers. And, once again, I've been privileged to have been on the "roads less travelled" but also know I've only touched the surface of this enormous country. I wouldn't think twice about coming back to do it all over again!

Tomorrow is another day, when we'll have to organise logistics to take the bike back, and I say my fond farewells and fly back to London. But, for right now, I'm enjoying the precious time with my dear new friends, and bottles of beer are clicked together, with us all shouting out "Cheers!"

16

DO JOURNEYS REALLY END?

Departure

The now only too familiar bright, early morning sunshine seeps through into my room for the last time, and I'm slowly woken up by the warm rays on my face. I smile. I look out and see the Florida year round blue skies and wonder what the weather's doing back in London, where I'll be by this time tomorrow. It's late October, and, no doubt, cold and drizzling with rain.

I turn over in the bed, not really wanting reality to hit quite so quickly today but already hear shuffling feet walking down the corridor to probably get the daily ritual started in getting the coffee on.

Ten minutes later, I hear a knock on my door. I'm right. "Coffee's brewed when you want it. Come on out to the garage when you're ready. We need to check stuff."

I wander into the silent, dark kitchen, where, as promised, Mike's kindly got the coffee ready. I take a mug from the shelf and pour it full, with just enough room to add some milk. It looks like the rest of the family is still asleep from the late night, so I quietly walk out to the veranda and look out to the empty baseballs fields with the seagulls flying overhead.

Out of sight, round the corner in the garage, I hear the sounds of banging and hammering going on, which is likely Mike endeavouring some kind of early morning job, which will of course be for one of his bikes.

I wander curiously over to see what else he's up to. "Hey. Morning, Mike. What you doing this bright and sunny morning?"

He's frowning. "More damn difficult than I thought. I had a job to find the screws we left when we took off your back seat rest before we went up to Alabama. Found them in the box. which had fallen behind those kids' baseball bats under the shelf. I remember you saying, before we set off, that you liked the bike to look streamline and minimalist and didn't think it looked too cool with the backrest on and just you riding it. I'm now trying to get the back rest back on before we take it to the guys in Lakeland later this morning. I've also checked the front windshield is secure, which we also took off up at Barber. All's fine. There shouldn't be any problems. The bike's looking good, considering it's done close to 2,000 miles since you took it."

He stands back from his work and gives a satisfied smile.

"Thanks, Mike. You needn't have. I was going to get it back on, but really appreciate it."

Again, from experience, I've learned never to say "no" to any sort of unasked for help and to be grateful for it. It will, for certain, have been done with kindness and generosity of spirit. Or maybe he's just impatient to get started and back on the road!

I sit on the grass outside, hugging my mug, and watch Mike continuing to potter around and then inflating the back tyre of his Bonneville.

"It's a pain, I know, you having to give the bike back today. You should have escaped and taken it over to the West Coast or somewhere you've never been before. And there are lots of those places here! How would they have found you?!"

I nod, slowly absorbing what he's saying, and smile. "Yea, I know. I could have escaped last night without a note and travelled up and down America where the weather's still good and maybe even down over the border!"

He smiles at the joke. "You know what they say: travelling and discovering new places gives you itchy feet to want more. We're a strange kind of people. Happy at home but always at some point wanting to get back onto the road and feel that freedom of no commitment to anyone but ourselves during the time we're away. It's not a selfish need, but it's still a need to keep us balanced and happy."

I consider his profound statements and lie back on the grass looking up at the sky. "I'm with you on that. You know me now. I've spent years living in different places and countries, and each time I take a big, challenging, or just different kind of trip, I tell myself that's all I'll ever need. But before I've even completed it, I'm thinking about where to next. So, you see, the journey of life never really finishes. But it also frustrates me knowing that life is going by so damn quick with so much still to see and do, and that I currently just don't have the resources or money to fulfil all the dreams I concoct. It sometimes saddens me when I hear the stories of those people who dream of travelling but can only do it from their armchair at home. I hope I'm not forced to become like that but, if I do, and have no money to do anything more, I won't regret a single thing I've done to see the world in a different way. What do they say, that 'you can't buy experiences, but money sure does help'?"

Mike finishes inflating his tyre and neatly rolls up the cable. "Yea. A bit like a drug, but a good one. I've put a bit extra in my tyres, 'cause you're gonna ride back with me once we've left your bike. Not that you're heavy, just something that has to be done," he chuckles.

"Plus, with Jacob on the back with me yesterday I just need to check that all's good to go. We'll take it nice and easy this morning getting up there and take the pretty route, like we did last time."

I nod, going with the flow. "You know, I said this to you all last night at the Chop House, that I really can't put into words what an eclectic trip this has been. I know the route wasn't one I'd have chosen and planned because I guess I just didn't know the alternative options, but I think maybe that's good. It made me a lot more open-minded and non-judgemental on what I saw. And, boy, it opened my eyes to so many extremes, from the poverty we saw in those places in the back of beyond in Alabama, where I really did think time had stood still, to the outward, materialistic decadence only just a bit further south in Sarasota and the west shore keys. And, hey, the diversity of the roads we biked along! I'll never forget those heavenly places along the Gulf of Mexico going up towards Panama City, with those beautiful beach houses standing on wooden stilts. Now that's the kind of place I'd like if I was a millionaire!

"They've all been fun and positive memories and experiences. And the people, well! Remember them all? We certainly did meet a diverse bunch of incredible people, all with so many stories to tell. Mr. Gip tortured by the Klu Klux Klan in Birmingham, Julie who sheltered us from the storm, the guys at Ace, and all those incidental and surprise encounters along the way."

I scratch my head, pulling more memories out, "Well, maybe some weren't so good, like encountering those prisoners in a chain gang working out in the forests in Alabama and riding through the storm in Georgia. But that's what's good. We certainly didn't get a sanitized, censored trip!"

"Hey, Zoë, you're getting deep and profound, like someone from the South. But, yea, I guess travelling does make you think like that, when everything else in your life is pushed to one side for a while. Things become clearer."

I nod, fully understanding. "And you guys know, like I've already said, that, if you want to come over, 'mi casa es tu casa.'"

Mike smiles in appreciation. "Gracias. Sure. That would be great. The idea of getting on a bike and riding up through the United Kingdom to some of your beautiful areas I've read about, like the Scottish Highlands, where they all wear kilts; seeing the Queen in Buckingham Palace; riding in the Wales countryside; and going to Liverpool, where the Beatles came from, would be one cool road trip. But I hear the roads aren't so big as here and there's a lot of roundabouts!"

I laugh at his possible irony. "Sure! They're big over there, too, but always very congested in and near the populated areas. The place is like one big network of roads. Remember, it's a small island with a lot of people, so we don't have a lot of room to stretch our arms out in certain places. But I guess, if you really wanted to kill yourself with exhaustion, you could get from the top to the bottom of England in a day. And, yes, up in remoter northern parts of England, like the Lake District, the Scottish Highlands, and Mid-Wales they're great for taking to the roads, with landscapes and terrain as good as here."

Mike wheels his bike out onto the grass next to me and, wiping his hand with a cloth, sits next to it as I continue, "But you know. One thing's for sure. It's further confirmed what I really want to get out of life or at least try to stop these continual stressful palpitations I get. I don't need the razzmatazz of jumping in and out of hoops of corporate politics and sorting out other people's mess at work anymore. Yea, I'm not afraid to work hard; always have; but I need a new direction, with fuller meaning than the current nine-to-five drudgery. Maybe I'm just talking too whimsically, but I'm going to take stock when I get back about how I can further cut back on stuff and find new ideas for a new direction. That's scary. That's another road trip of life! But they do say, 'It's good not to know our destiny.' It makes us work harder to get what we want."

Chatting away like that, time seems to have gone by maybe a bit too quickly, and soon the kids are shouting from inside. "Are we going to see Zoë before she leaves after we get back from school?"

Walking back inside, Mike smiles gently. "Unfortunately," he sighs, "We've soon gotta get the bike back up to Lakeland. We'll head back here on mine and should be back within the next few hours. But then we gotta pick her luggage and stuff up from here, where I'll be taking her to the airport in VIP style!" He winks at the kids, and I look inquisitively back.

"Yes, I forgot to say, you're in for a treat. When we get back I'm going to bike over to my father-in-law's and collect his Lincoln Towncar to drive us to the airport in true limo style. But, I promise you, if I'd had a side-car, we'd have done it in that!"

For one last time, I push the black beauty out of the garage and, with nothing to pack onto it, just take a cloth from the now empty side bag and gently polish the black tank. I stand back, and the sun bounces back off it, creating a glistening shine. It looks good.

With nothing left to do, we start the bikes up and hear the sound of both engines purring in contented harmony.

Then Mike nods, and we're off. I push my foot down, clicking into first gear, and slowly follow him out of the driveway and past the playing fields, kick my foot lever up into second, then third past the lake, up and over the railway tracks, and out of Lake Wales to Lakeland.

There's a very good reason that both towns have water-related names. The entire area between them, here in the middle of Florida, is dotted with hundreds of lakes of every conceivable size.

We're soon out on one of the many small, quiet and empty country roads that only the locals would really use, with the orange groves on either side and with the sound of bird song somewhere up in the trees. I smile for the umpteenth time and breathe in deeply the warm morning air, trying to smell those citrus fruit and imagining what their sweet taste must be like from all this warm, year-long sunshine.

Then we're slowly going round a bend in the road and coming to the first of many of the lakes in the area, some with boats moored up on the banks and others with pretty homes overlooking them. Some of the lakes names make sense and some simply no sense at all and must have been just simply the names of the people that were the first to live here: Effie, Padgett, Mountain Lodge, Tater Patch, Bess, Ruby, Winterset, Eloise, Lulu, Shipp, May, Howard, Hancock, Eagle, Crystal, Millsite, Spirit, Bonny, Banana, Little Banana, and, of course, what else but Horney Lake! Maybe that one has seen a bit of action in or on it.

But it's the feeling of joy, which I will never forget, of riding down the small roads and being greeted by the true Deep South, with its humble but proud residences and lined as far as the eye can see with the beautiful Spanish moss covered trees—the majestic trees on either side of the roads all adorned heavily with the long, dangling moss swaying so gently in the warm breeze and some ultimately brushing the ground below. They make it feel like a very special, hidden place that hasn't changed for a long, long time.

Reality is literally just round the corner, on East Memorial Boulevard, to be exact, as we come to a busy intersection and cross over to the Fun Bike Center in Lakeland. The black beauty is carefully parked up at the front, and the keys handed back. Not a single scratch, dent, or mark on it. After indebted thanks to the guys, Mike simply starts his Bonnie back up again, indicating with a twist of his head that I jump on the back, and we've disappeared back down the silent lanes.

In a wink of an eye, we're parked up, back at the house. I swing my leg over and get off.

Mike smiles, still on his bike. "Just so you know, Zoë, I'm running down to my father-in-laws now to get that courtesy limo I talked about to get you back in style. Get your bags ready, and then we'll be ready to head out when I get back."

True to his word, a short while later, a massive, beautiful, champagne-coloured Lincoln Towncar arrives. I open the passenger door and melt into the cream, embossed leather seat.

"All we have to do now is get you to the Orlando airport on time. No more adventures for us today, but we sure can talk about the next ones."

I smile, nodding, thinking that sounds like the best idea of the day.

APPENDIX

Just some of the interesting and recommended places to eat and unique places to visit found on this road trip through Florida, Alabama, and Georgia.

Bessemer, AL
Gip's Place, 3101 Ave. C, Bessemer—historic juke joint, www.gipsplace.org—best to go with someone who's been there before and knows how to get there. There's no telephone number to call, but you can check the MySpace site for GipsJukeJoint to see if bands are playing on Saturday night.

Birmingham and Leeds, AL
Hampton Inn Birmingham, 310 Rex Lake Road, Leeds 35094—205-702-4141—the closest hotel to the Barber Museum and Motorsport Park

Barber Vintage Motorsports Museum and Barber Motorsports Park, 6030 Barber Motorsports Parkway, Birmingham, AL 35094, www.barbermuseum.org

Logan's Roadhouse Restaurant, 1999 Village Drive, Leeds 35094—205-640-5237—steak rules here, plus seafood and great bar

Ruby Tuesday, 2023 Village Drive, Leeds 35094—great casual chain with burgers

Daytona Beach, FL
Joe's Crab Shack, 1200 Main Street (on the Pier), Daytona Beach 32118—386-238 4050, www.joescrabshack.com

Biketoberfest, www.biketoberfest.org—386-255-0415

Daytona International Speedway, 1801 West International Speedway Boulevard, Daytona—800-748-7467, www.daytonaintlspeedway.com

Frostproof, FL
Frostproof Family Restaurant, 133 S. Scenic Hwy—863-635-6595

Jasper, FL
The Pecan Outlet, 8196 State Road 6 W, Jasper 32052 (exit 460 off Interstate 75)

Lakeland, FL
Fun Bike Center Motorsports, 1845 E. Memorial Drive, Lakeland, FL 33801—863-688-3333

Lake Wales, FL
Lake Wailes Park, on the shores of Lake Wailes

Bok Tower Gardens, 1151 Tower Blvd, Lake Wales 33853, www.boktowergardens.org

Crooked Lake (five miles south of Lake Wales on east side of US Hwy 27)

Spook Hill, North Wales Drive, Lake Wales 33853—a gravity hill—optical illusion where cars appear to roll up the hill!

Mannys Original Chop House, 210 State Road 60W, Lake Wales 33853—863-678-0370

Longboat Key, FL
Sandpiper Inn, 5451 Gulf of Mexico Drive, Longboat Key, FL 34228—941-383-2552, innkeeper@sandpiperinn.com

Blue Dolphin Cafe, 5370 Gulf of Mexico Drive, Longboat Key, FL 34228—941-383-3787

The Dry Dock Waterfront Grill, 412 Gulf of Mexico Drive, Longboat Key 34228—941-383-0102

Publix Supermarket, 525 Bay Isles Parkway, Longboat Key, FL 34228

Manchester, GA
Tant's Cafe, 250 W. Main Street, Manchester 31816

President Cinema—Main Street; authentic Art Deco building

Orlando, FL
Ace Cafe USA, W. Livingston Street, Orlando 32801, www.acecafeusa.com

London
Ace Cafe, Ace Corner, North Circular Road, Stonebridge, London NW10 7UD - UK—Tel: 020 8961 1000, www.ace-cafe-london.com

AIMExpo

The Annual American International Motorcycle Exposition, Orlando's Orange County Convention Center (OCCC), 9899 International Drive, Orlando 32819, www.occc.net

Panama City, FL

Billy's Oyster Bar & Crab House, 3000 Thomas Dr. Panama City Beach 32408, www.billysoysterbar.com

Sarasota, FL

Columbia Restaurant, 411 St Armands Circle, Sarasota 34236—941-388-3987

Vernon, FL

Dee's Restaurant, 3730 FL 277, Vernon 32462, www.deesrestaruantvernonfl.com

Vincent, AL

Twisting 20 mile road heading to Leeds, AL 25N—mini Dragon's Tail

Final Mileage

Bikes used

2014 Triumph Bonneville T100 865 cc
2011 Triumph Bonneville T100 865 cc

Mileage

Day 1—Lake Wales, FL to Panama City, FL; 392 miles
Day 2—Panama City, FL to Leeds, AL; 346 miles
Day 3—Barber Vintage Show, Leeds, AL
Day 4—Barber Vintage Show, Leeds, AL
Day 5—Barber Vintage Show, Leeds, AL
Day 6—Leeds, AL to Valdosta, GA; 350 miles
Day 7—Valdosta, GA to Lake Wales, FL; 240 miles
Day 8—Lake Wales, FL to Longboat, FL; 110 miles

Day 9—Longboat Key, FL to Sarasota, FL; just a couple of miles

Day 10—Longboat Key, FL back to Lake Wales, FL; 114 miles

Day 11—Lake Wales, FL to Orlando, FL & back to Lake Wales; 88 miles

Day 12—Lake Wales, FL to Downtown Orlando, FL & back; 102 miles

Day 13—Lake Wales, FL to Daytona Beach, FL & back to Lake Wales; 228 miles

Day 14—Lake Wales, FL to Lakeland,FL; 28 miles

ACKNOWLEDGEMENTS

As I'm beginning to see, road trips like this one can't be done totally on their own, and the generous help and support received this time have been phenomenal.

A massive thank you to my friend, Mike Fitterling, for your enthusiasm to join the adventure. The trip wouldn't have happened without the big push and volunteering to be my "Road Dog" travelling companion for a large part of the journey, kindly providing accommodation with your family and friends, assisting with the navigation, and getting us safely up to Birmingham, Alabama.

I would personally like to convey my gratitude to everyone at Triumph Motorcycles USA in Atlanta, including Matt Sheahan, Jess Giesen, and Steve Bidlack, for generously helping to source the Triumph Bonneville T100 for me and welcoming me to be with them at the highly successful Barber Vintage Festival 2014. Everyone at Fun Bike Center Motorsports, Lakeland, Florida, particularly Elliott Dorsch, Samer Fidy, and Nicholas Dorsch, for providing the Triumph Bonneville for the *Southern Escapades* road trip and your warm welcome. Even the colour of the bike was perfect!

On this side of the pond, in England, I'd like to express my gratitude to Gareth Bright and Andrea Friggi at Triumph Motorcycles Ltd. Wonderful Mark and Linda Wilsmore of The Ace Cafe, London, for their generous help and support in providing valuable details of the Cafe's history. Mark McKee and Steve Glum of Ace Cafe USA, for providing insightful information on the new Ace Cafe venture in Orlando.

Julie and Jack Bowland for sheltering us from the storm in Valdosta. Andrew Keel for showing us the sights in Panama City.

Robin Dail, of Moto Girl Café, for kindly inviting me onto her stand at Ace Corner at Barber for more book signings. Great fun! Breeann Poland, with her incredible interviewing style, and the guys, Jason and Herm from Dime City Cycles, for their great welcome at Ace Corner. Mr. Gip and Melissa Veitch at Gip's Place, Bessemer, and Matt Marshall from *American Blues Scene Magazine*, for the introduction. Matt Frey and his team from British Customs, Los Angeles, for checking our bikes at Barber before returning to Florida. Lindsay Chong of Hedon Helmets.

Many thanks to Rich and Gary from RokStraps, for your spontaneous hospitality at your booth at AIMExpo. Enjoyed the laughs! "Guzzi" Steve from Cafe Racer Podcast, for the great coverage.

Dave and the team at Jack Lilley Triumph, London, for your continued support.

And once again, to my wonderful friend, Paul Roberts, for another jaw dropping book cover.

Zoë writes the blog bonnevilleadventure.blogspot.com while twittering at @bijoulatina.

Also by Zoë Cano & from Road Dog Publications

Bonneville Go or Bust

★★★★★
Reviews from Amazon

"The sheer grit & determination of this woman to achieve her dream bounces off every page"

"Simply amazing! A story written with great verve & passion"

"Out of the box travelling. Full of excitement"

"You want to be on the bike with her & by reading this you are along for the ride!"

"Motorcycle adventure + travelogue + personal discovery = winning combination"

"A thrill ride on two wheels— an up-close-and-personal tour of Americana"

"It's like riding on the back of the bike with her with the wind in your hair, exploring this amazing country"

In life we all have dreams. But do we ever attempt to make them happen?

A true story with a difference. She had nothing. No money. No time. No motorbike. No experience for such a mammoth trip. But she did have a clear vision. So with gritted determination, she goes all out to make her dream come true: to travel solo and unassisted across the lesser-known roads of the North American continent covering more than 8,000 km on a classic Triumph Bonneville.

From the outset to the end of this escapade, it's always going to be a question of "Go or Bust" on whether she'll ever succeed or even finish the journey with the most unexpected obstacles, dangers and surprises that come her way. Her wry sense of humour helps without doubt, get her out of some of anyone's worst case scenarios.

An inspiring and motivational story written with passion to succeed against all odds, a true life lesson in believing in yourself— there is no such thing as dreaming too big.

So let the adventure begin!

Other Books from
—Road Dog Publications—

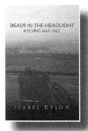

Beads in the Headlight

A British couple tackle riding from Alaska to Tierra del Fuego two-up on a 31 year-old BMW "airhead." Join them on this adventure of a lifetime across two continents.

A great blend of travel, motorcycling, determination, and humor.   —Dee (★★★★★ Amazon Review)

A Short Ride in the Jungle

The true story of a woman riding the Ho Chi Minh Trail alone on a Honda C90. An epic ride on a vintage Japanese motorcyle, filled with adventure and history.

Truly wonderful...a lovely book, very much after my own heart.—Ted Simon, author of *Jupiter's Travels*

Motorcycles, Life, and...
The Elemental Motorcyclist

Two books by award winning riding instructor and creator of the popular "Howzit Done?" video series, Brent "Capt. Crash" Allen. Thoughts about riding and life and how they combine told in a lighthearted and informative tone.

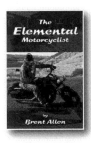

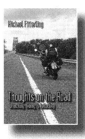

Thoughts on the Road

The founder of Road Dog Publications and Editor of *Vintage Japanese Motorcycle Magazine*, ponders his experience with motorcycles & riding, and how those two things intersect and influence his life.

A Tale of Two Dusters & Other Stories

In this collection of tales Kirk Swanick tells of growing up a gear head behind both the wheels of muscle cars and the handlebars of motorcycles and describes the joys and trials of riding.

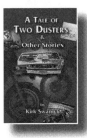